BECOMING
BEN FRANKLIN

ALSO BY RUSSELL FREEDMAN

BECOMING BEN FRANKLIN

How a Candle-Maker's
Son Helped Light
the Flame of Liberty

RUSSELL FREEDMAN

HOLIDAY HOUSE · NEW YORK

Text copyright © 2013 by Russell Freedman
All Rights Reserved
HOLIDAY HOUSE is registered in the U.S. Patent and Trademark Office.
Printed and bound in March 2021 at C&C Offset, Shenzhen, China.
The text typeface is Caslon Old Face.
www.holidayhouse.com
First Edition
3 5 7 9 10 8 6 4 2

Library of Congress Cataloging-in-Publication Data
Freedman, Russell.
Becoming Ben Franklin / Russell Freedman. — 1st ed.
p. cm.
ISBN 978-0-8234-2374-3 (hardcover)
1. Franklin, Benjamin, 1706–1790—Juvenile literature.   2. Statesmen—United States—Biography—Juvenile literature.
3. Inventors—United States—Biography—Juvenile literature.   4. Scientists—United States—Biography—Juvenile literature.
5. Printers—United States—Biography—Juvenile literature.   I. Title.
E302.6.F8F8495 2013
973.3092—dc23
[B]
2012002971
ISBN: 978-0-8234-2374-3 (hardcover)
ISBN: 978-0-8234-4945-3 (paperback)

To Bob Hershon and Donna Brook

Printers, Publishers, Poets

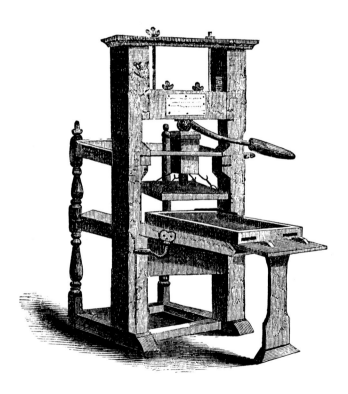

CONTENTS

 *Chapter One*

The Runaway Apprentice

Benjamin Franklin, seventeen years old with a mind of his own, stepped ashore in Philadelphia and headed up Market Street. He had been traveling ten days by sea and land—walking part of the way, drenched by rain, sleeping at night in crowded inns—since running away from his family and his job as a printer's apprentice in Boston.

"I was dirty from my journey," he remembered. "My pockets were stuffed out with shirts and stockings; I knew no soul, nor where to look for lodging. I was fatigued with traveling, rowing and want of rest. I was very hungry, and my whole stock of cash consisted of a Dutch dollar and about a shilling in copper."

He offered to pay the boatmen who had dropped him off at the Market Street wharf early on a Sunday morning. They refused, since he had helped row the boat. "But I insisted on them taking it, a man being sometimes more generous when he has but little money than when he has plenty, perhaps through fear of being thought to have little."

Then he set out to find something to eat—a spunky lad bounding with energy and ambition, "well set and very strong," as he described himself. He had broad shoulders, a swimmer's chest, a winning smile, and a healthy appetite.

He found a bakery and bought three big, puffy rolls for a penny each, but "having no room in my pockets, walked off with a roll under each arm, and eating the other." One roll was enough for the time being. He gave the other two to a woman and her child he had met on the boat.

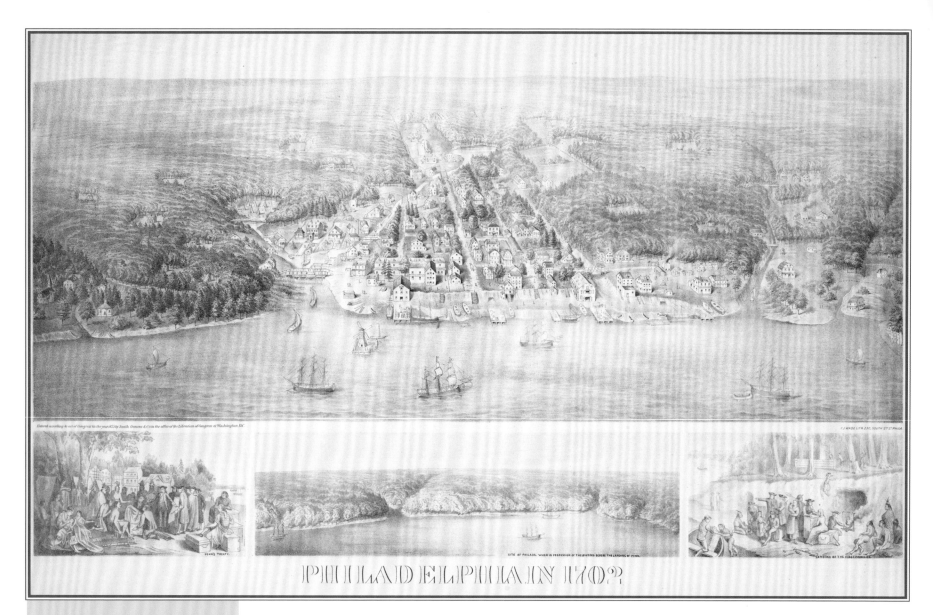

PHILADELPHIA IN 1702

Philadelphia in 1702. By the time Ben Franklin arrived in 1723, the population had grown to two thousand, making Philadelphia America's second-largest town after Boston.

Gazing about, he noticed a young girl standing in the doorway of her father's house. Fifteen-year-old Deborah Read—his future wife—returned his glance, and, as he later learned, "thought I made as I most certainly did a most awkward ridiculous appearance."

By now, lots of well-dressed people had appeared on Market Street. They were all walking in the same direction. Ben followed them to a Quaker meetinghouse nearby. "I sat down among them, and after looking around awhile and hearing nothing said, being very drowsy through labor and want of rest the preceding night, I fell fast asleep, and continued so till the meeting broke up, when one was kind enough to arouse me."

As Ben left the meetinghouse, he asked where he might find a proper meal and lodging for the night. He was directed to the Crooked Billet, a tavern and inn on King Street. While he was eating, "several sly questions were asked me, as it seemed to be suspected from my youth and appearance, that I might be some runaway." But no one challenged him. After a satisfying supper, he went to bed "very early and slept soundly till the next morning."

Then he set out to seek his first job as an independent young man.

* * *

Before running off to Philadelphia, young Ben Franklin had never spent a night away from Boston, where he was born on January 17, 1706. He was the fifteenth of seventeen children and the youngest son of a soap and candle maker. Growing up in a household overflowing with brothers and sisters older than himself, he learned early to get along with others. Though some of his older siblings were gone by the time Ben appeared, he remembered thirteen children sitting down at one time at his father's table.

An artist's impression of Ben as a teenager and as a mature man.

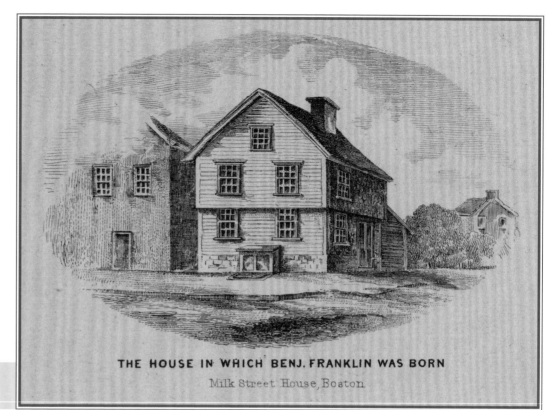

THE HOUSE IN WHICH BENJ. FRANKLIN WAS BORN

Milk Street House, Boston

Franklin's birthplace on Milk Street in Boston.

Boston was the biggest town in colonial America and the busiest seaport, home to more than a thousand sailing ships that plied the trade routes between the New World and the Old. The tangy smell of salt air hung over the town, and from his doorstep, a block from the water, Ben could see tall masts with sails furled lined up beside the town's Long Wharf.

"Living near the water, I was much in and about it, learned early to swim well, and to manage boats," he recalled in his autobiography. Wishing to swim faster, he made wooden paddles for his hands, with holes for his thumbs, and wooden flippers for his feet, which he attached like "a kind of sandals." The more water he could push with his hands and feet, he figured, the faster he could propel himself forward. But his experiment failed. The hand paddles were too heavy and tired his wrists, and the flippers were too stiff to do much good.

His swimming experiment with a kite was more successful. Sending a kite aloft on a windy day, he held on to the string, waded into a pond, floated on his back, and let the kite pull him along. "I began to cross the pond with my kite," he told a friend, "which carried me quite over without the least fatigue and with the greatest pleasure imaginable."

Ben was fond of dreaming up projects and organizing his friends to carry out his plans. "I was generally a leader among the boys," he wrote, "and sometimes led them into scrapes." He liked to fish with his friends for minnows in a salt marsh along the Charles River, but their constant trampling had turned the marsh into a muddy quagmire. Ben's bright idea was to build themselves a stone wharf to stand on, drawing from a big pile of building stones intended for the construction of a house nearby.

"In the evening, when the workmen were gone, I assembled a number of my playfellows, and

The town of Boston as seen from the harbor, c. 1730.

working with them…sometimes two or three to a stone…built our little wharf." When the workmen returned the next morning and found their missing stones piled up at the boys' wharf, the culprits were discovered and punished. Ben pleaded that at least they had built something useful, but his father "convinced me that nothing was useful that was not honest."

Clever as he was, Ben had only two years of schooling before he started full-time work as an apprentice. Most boys in colonial America had little more than that, while most girls had no formal schooling at all. At his grammar school, Ben excelled in writing, which wasn't surprising since he loved to read. "I do not remember when I could not read," he later wrote. But he proved slow at doing sums and failed arithmetic twice, a deficiency he would try to remedy later through home study. At the age of ten, he left his school days behind and became an apprentice in the soap- and candle-making shop of his father, Josiah.

Soap and candles were essential to colonial life, but making them was a hot, messy, smelly job. Tallow was skimmed from a boiling vat of animal fat and poured into molds. Ben was put to work stirring the smoking vats, filling the molds, cutting wicks for candles, tending the shop, and running errands. Josiah recognized that the boy was increasingly bored and restless. He worried that Ben would "break away and get to sea," as his eldest brother, Josiah Jr., had done years earlier. Josiah Jr. had been lost at sea when his ship went down in a storm, and Ben's father could not bear the thought of losing his youngest son in the same way.

Josiah gave up the idea of training Ben as a soap and candle maker. He began to take his son on walks around town to visit other craftsmen at work, as Ben explained, "that he might observe my inclination, and endeavor to fix it on some trade or other on land. It has ever since been a pleasure to me to see good workmen handle their tools, and it has been useful to me, having learned so much by it, as to be able to do little jobs myself in my home."

Ben's brother James had recently set himself up as a printer, and Ben's "bookish inclination," as he himself described it, "determined my father to make me a printer." The printing trade required the ability to read, spell, and write, skills Ben had mastered. And he was strong enough to haul trays of lead type and operate the heavy wooden press. So it was settled. Ben signed up to work for his brother without pay for an unusually long apprenticeship of nine years. He was twelve years old. He would be free to strike out on his own when he was twenty-one.

Young Ben Franklin the printer, as imagined in this 1914 painting by Charles Mills.

"In a little time I made a great proficiency in the business, and became a useful hand to my brother," Franklin wrote. The smell of printer's ink, the thump of the wooden press, the sucking sound of sheets of paper emerging from the press became part of the teenager's daily life.

As a printer's apprentice, he made friends with a bookseller's apprentice, who allowed Ben to borrow books after he finished work. "Often I sat up in my room reading the greatest part of the night, when the book was borrowed in the evening and to be returned early in the morning lest it should be missed or wanted."

About this time, Ben came across a bound volume of *The Spectator*, a popular London journal that published essays by some of the best writers of the day. "I had never before seen any of them. I bought it, read it over and over, and was much delighted with it. I thought the writing excellent, and wished if possible to imitate it." To improve his own writing, he would take notes on the meaning of an essay, lay the notes aside, and after a few days, working only with his notes, try to re-create the original essay "as fully as it had been expressed before, in any suitable words, that should come to hand. Then I compared my Spectator with the original, discovered some of my faults, and corrected them."

To improve his "stock of words or a readiness in recollecting and using them," he would turn

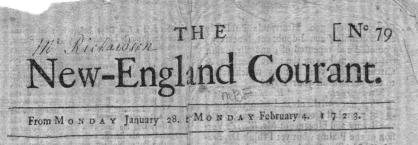

THE   [N° 79]

New-England Courant.

From MONDAY January 28. to MONDAY February 4. 1723.

In France, and other Nations, the meer Will of the Prince is Law: His Word takes off any Man's Head, imposes Taxes, seizes any man's Estate, when, how, and as often as he lists; And if one be accused, or but so much as suspected of any Crime, he may either presently execute him, or banish, or imprison him at Pleasure. *English Liberties Page 1.*

To the Author of the New-England Courant.

SIR,

FIND it was a heinous Crime in old King Alfred's Days, not only to condemn a Man without Action or Answer, but also to punish him against Law, where there was no Law provided. "King "Alfred * caused Forty "Four Judges in one "Year, to be hanged as "Murderers for their "false *Judgments.* He hanged *Seafoul,* because he "judged *Ording* to Death without *Answer.* He "hanged *Rambold,* because he judged *Lesebild* it a "Case not notorious, without *Appeal,* and without "*Indictment.* He hanged *Athulf,* because he caus'd "*Copping* to be hanged before the Age of one and "twenty Years, it being —— "for nought else but because he taught to him who "vanquished him by *Battle-mortal,* to say the Word "*Cravant.*"

This last Instance of Justice in King *Alfred,* may be thought worthy our particular Notice. The Word *Cravant* us'd formerly to be pronounced by those who were vanquished in a Tryal by Battel; By which we may suppose, that this *Frankling* was an ill-natur'd Fellow, who study'd the Art of Quarrelling, and setting his Town and Country together by the Ears, under Pretence of instructing them in Manly Exercises for the Defence of their *Liberties:* And yet, he was no doubt a meer Coward, a mean spirited, base Fellow, and a scandal to his Country; for when he had been *sorely bang'd,* and vanquish'd in Battle, he took the Advantage of his Conqueror's Ignorance, and taught him to say *Cravant,* when he should have said it himself. But notwithstanding this *Frankling* might deserve *Hanging,* and it was perhaps said of him, that *it was a thousand Pities he was born in England;* yet there being no Law then in Force against his *teaching the Word Cravant,* —— him, lest it should be made a Precedent towards for condemning Men *without Law.*

A Manuscript has lately been found in the Street, and accidentally come to my Hands, wherein this Case seems to be set in a true Light. It appears to be the rough Draught of a Letter to some Honourable Person; and I here send it you to publish or conceal, as you think proper, and remain, *SIR,* Your Humble Servant, JULA.

SIR,

I Am inform'd that your Honour was a leading Man in the late Extraordinary procedure against F——n the Printer. And inasmuch as it cannot be long before you must appear at *Christ's* enlightned Tri-

bunal, where every Man's work shall be tryed, I humbly beseech you, in the Fear of God, to consider & Examine, whether that Procedure be according to *the strict Rules of Justice and Equity?* It is manifest, that this Man had broke no Law; and you know, Sir, that where there is no Law, there can be no Transgression: And, Sir, methinks you cannot but know, that it is highly *unjust* to punish a Man by a Law, to which the Fact committed is *antecedent.* The Law ever looks *forward,* but never *backward;* but if once we come to punish Men, by vertue of Laws *Ex post facto,* Farewel *Magna Charta,* and *English Liberties,* for no Man can ever be *safe,* but may be punished for every Action he does by Laws made afterwards. This in my humble Opinion, both the Light of Nature and Laws of Justice abhor, and is what ought to be detested by all Good Men.

Summum jus, est summa injuria.

Moreover, this is not according to the procedure of the *supream Judge of all the Earth,* —— is the most perfect Rule for *Humane Gods* to copy after. You know, Sir, that he will Judge and punish Men, according to that *Light and Law* they were favour'd with; And that he will not punish the *Heathen* for disobeying th' Gospel, of which they were intirely ignorant.

The end of Humane Law is to fix the boundaries within which Men ought to keep themselves; But if any are so hardy and presumptuous as to break through them, doubtless they deserve punishment. Now, If this *Printer* had transgress'd any Law, he ought to have been presented by a Grand Jury, and a fair Tryal brought on.

I would further observe to your Honour the danger of ill Precedents, and that this Bear to think that Posterity will have Reason to Curse you on the Account hereof! By this our Religion may suffer extreamly hereafter; for, whatever those Ministers (if any such there were) who have push'd on this matter, may think of it, they have made a Rod for themselves in times to come, Blessed be God, we have a good King at present; but if it should please him for our Sins to punish us with a bad one, we may have a S——y that will so *Supervise* our Ministers Sermons, as to suffer them to print none at all.

I would also humbly remind your Honour, that you were formerly led into a

+ See *Mirrour of Justices,* p. 239.

---

some of the essays into verse, and after he had pretty much forgotten the prose, turn them back again. Or he would jumble his notes on an essay into confusion, and after a few weeks, try to reorganize them. "This was to teach me method in the arrangement of thoughts. By comparing my work afterwards with the original, I discovered many faults and amended them; but I sometimes had the pleasure of fancying that in certain particulars of small import, I had been lucky enough to improve the method or the language and this encouraged me to think I might possibly in time come to be a tolerable English writer, of which I was extremely ambitious."

Ben had a chance to try out his self-taught writing style when his brother James began to publish a newspaper, *The New-England Courant.* James invited his friends to contribute articles, and Ben, listening to them praise one another's work, "was excited to try my hand among them." But he suspected that his brother would "object to presenting anything of mine in his paper if he knew it to be mine." Ben, after all, was a lowly apprentice, a boy of sixteen.

Disguising his handwriting, Ben wrote a humorous piece, signed it "Silence Dogood," a fictitious woman's name, and slipped it under the printing-house door. Writing under an assumed name was a common practice at the time, especially among authors who wanted to express unpopular views.

Ben's first published essays, written when he was sixteen, appeared in his brother James's newspaper, The New-England Courant.

When James's writer friends gathered at the shop the next day, Ben had the "exquisite pleasure" of hearing them praise *his* work and try to guess who Silence Dogood might actually be. His essay was published. It proved so popular that Ben wrote fourteen Silence Dogood essays in all, poking fun at the foibles and pretensions of Boston society.

When James found out that Silence Dogood was in fact his precocious youngest brother, he wasn't pleased, "as he thought, probably with reason," that all the praise the essays were receiving "tended to make me too vain." They began to quarrel. "Though a brother, he considered himself as my master, and me as his apprentice…while I thought he demeaned me too much."

"Perhaps I was too saucy and provoking," Franklin later admitted. His behavior incited James to beat Ben, "which I took extremely amiss, and thinking my apprenticeship very tedious, I was continually wishing for some opportunity of shortening it."

The brothers called a truce when James got into trouble. He offended the Boston authorities by printing articles criticizing the government. Jailed for a month and forbidden to publish his paper, James evaded the order by naming Ben as publisher of the *Courant.* The issue of February 11, 1723, announced: "Printed and sold by BENJAMIN FRANKLIN in Queen Street where ADVERTISEMENTS are taken."

When James was released from jail and allowed to resume his editorship, fresh differences flared up between the brothers. "His harsh and tyrannical treatment," Franklin wrote, "[impressed] me with that aversion to arbitrary power that has stuck to me through my whole life." Determined to escape Boston and make his way in the world, "I took it upon me to assert my freedom."

Ben sold some of his books to raise money, and with the help of a friend, secretly booked passage on a sloop sailing to New York.

"As we had a fair wind in three days I found myself in New York nearly 300 miles from home, a boy of but seventeen, without the least recommendation to or knowledge of any person in the place, and with very little money in my pocket."

Failing to find a job in New York, he set out for Philadelphia, a five-day journey by boat and on foot, including a fifty-mile hike across New Jersey in heavy rain. The last stage of his journey was up the Delaware River in a large rowboat, which carried him the rest of the way to Philadelphia.

Chapter Two

Benjamin Franklin of Philadelphia, Printer

As an ambitious young Philadelphia printer, Franklin often carted the paper he purchased for his press through the streets to his shop in a wheelbarrow.

Philadelphia was a small town, and Ben had no trouble settling in and making friends. People were drawn to him. And Ben, for his part, enjoyed the company of others. He had a quick wit and a talent for storytelling. "I lived very agreeably," he recalled, "forgetting Boston as much as I could."

He found work at the printing shop of Samuel Keimer, a disheveled and talkative man who owned a broken-down press, which Ben dismantled and repaired. "I endeavored to put his press into order fit to be worked with," he recalled. And he rented a room in the Market Street home of John Read, father of Deborah, the girl who had laughed at him from her doorway as he walked up Market Street with a puffy roll under each arm.

His new friends included three young clerks, "lovers of reading, with whom I spent my evenings very pleasantly." They shared Ben's writing ambitions. "Many pleasant walks we four had together on Sundays into the woods near Skuylkill, where read to one another and conferred on what we read."

When Pennsylvania Governor William Keith heard about this bright and amiable teenager from Boston, he called at Keimer's shop and introduced himself to Ben. "He said I appeared a young man of promising parts, and therefore should be encouraged." Governor Keith had a low opinion of the two printers then working in Philadelphia.

He was convinced that Ben knew more about printing than anyone else in town, "and if I would set up there, he [had] no doubt I should succeed." Keith offered to help the young newcomer establish his own printing shop if Ben's father would agree to finance the venture.

So seven months after he had run away, Ben returned to Boston, carrying a letter from Governor Keith "saying many flattering things of me to my father, and strongly recommending the project of my setting up at Philadelphia."

His parents "were very glad to see me and made me welcome," though his brother James was cool when Ben showed up at his printing shop. "I was better dressed than ever while in his service, having a genteel new suit from head to foot, a watch, and my pockets lined with near five pounds sterling in silver." James looked his former apprentice over, then turned silently back to work. But his young employees crowded around, eager to ask about life in faraway Philadelphia, impressed by Ben's fine suit of clothes, by his watch, and by the pocketful of silver coins he spread out on a table before them.

Ben's father was pleased that his son had done so well in Philadelphia, but he wasn't ready to finance Ben's printing venture, "I being in his opinion too young to be trusted with the management of a business so important and for which the preparations must be so expensive." If Ben could save almost enough to open his own shop by the time he was twenty-one, then, Josiah promised, he would help out with the rest.

Back in Philadelphia, Governor Keith offered to put up the money. "Since he will not set you up," said Keith, "I will do it myself.... You shall repay me when you are able. I am resolved to have a good printer here, and I am sure you must succeed."

Sir William Keith, royal governor of Pennsylvania. He made promises he couldn't keep.

Ben figured he would need about one hundred pounds sterling to buy a printing press, type, and other equipment, all of which had to be shipped from England. Keith then suggested that Ben sail to London, where he could personally pick out the equipment he needed and at the same time meet some London booksellers and stationers. "I agreed that this might be advantageous. Then, says he, get yourself ready to go." The governor promised to supply a letter of credit to pay for both the voyage and the printing equipment, along with letters to his London friends recommending Ben.

Ben set sail for England aboard the *London Hope*, arriving on Christmas Eve, 1724, after a seven-week voyage from Philadelphia. But when the ship's captain unsealed the bag of mail he had carried across the Atlantic, Ben could not find a single letter of credit or recommendation from Governor Keith.

A fellow passenger, Thomas Denham, told Ben "there was not the least probability that [Keith] had written any letters for me, that no one who knew him had the smallest dependence on him, and he laughed at the notion of the governor's giving me a letter of credit, having as he said no credit to give." Keith, as Franklin now discovered, was notorious for his impulsive enthusiasms and for making promises he could not keep.

"What shall we think of a governor's playing such pitiful tricks, and imposing so grossly on a poor ignorant boy!" Franklin exclaimed. "It was a habit he had acquired. He wished to please everybody, and having little to give, he gave expectations."

Denham advised Ben to make the best of his situation and find work with a London printer. "You will improve yourself," Denham told him, "and when you return to America, you will set up to greater advantage."

London was the great throbbing metropolis at the heart of the far-flung British Empire, which included England's thirteen American colonies. The city had a population of over half a million, dwarfing Philadelphia and every other town in colonial America. Ben easily found work at one of London's many printing houses. A muscular nineteen-year-old now, he kept in shape by carrying two sets of heavy type, one in each hand, while running up and down the printing-house steps. Meanwhile he found cheap lodgings, arranged to borrow books from a neighborhood bookseller, flirted with pretty English girls, and "spent a good deal of my earnings going to plays and other places of amusement."

Ben was as sociable in teeming, sophisticated London as he had been in sleepy, small-town Philadelphia. Never shy, he sought out coffeehouses and taverns where he could meet writers and other interesting people, and he made friends at every turn. With growing confidence, he wrote an ambitious essay called *A Dissertation on Liberty and Necessity, Pleasure and Pain*, printed a hundred copies, and handed them out. An author named William Lyons, impressed by Ben's writing, "took great notice of me, called on me often, to converse on [various] topics," and introduced Ben to his circle of intellectual friends.

In an era when most people, even sailors, could not swim, Ben gave swimming lessons to some of his fellow printers. During a Sunday boat trip on the Thames, he showed off by stripping, diving in, and swimming from Chelsea to Blackfriars, a distance of at least two miles, "performing on the

58 Queen-Hithe.
59 St. Mary Somerset.
60 St. Mary Magdalen.
61 St. Nicholas Cole Abby.
62 St. Pauls Cathedral.
63 St. Michaels Queen-Hithe.
64 Three Crane Stairs.
65 St. Austin's.
66 Christ Church.
67 St. Mildreds.
68 St. James's Garlick Hill.
69 St. Mathew's.
70 St. Vedest alias.
71 St. Foster's.
72 Allhallow's Breadstreet.
72
73
74

Ben was eighteen when he sailed to London, capital of the British Empire. Engraving by Samuel and Nathaniel Buck, 1749.

way many feats of activity both upon and under water, that surprised and pleased those to whom they were novelties."

Ben spent eighteen months in London. As much as he enjoyed the city, he became homesick. He "remembered with pleasure the happy months I had spent in Pennsylvania, and wished again to see it." In July of 1726, he sailed back to America aboard the *Berkshire*. Once they had caught a favorable wind and put to sea, he amused himself and astounded his fellow passengers by diving overboard and swimming around the ship.

✳   ✳   ✳

Back in Philadelphia, Franklin worked briefly for his old boss Samuel Keimer, then went into business with a partner. By the time he was twenty-four, he had saved enough money to open his own shop. He quickly earned a reputation as the most skillful and industrious printer in town. "The industry of that Franklin is superior to anything I ever saw," a neighbor remarked. "I see him at work when I go home [at night], and he is at work again before his neighbors are out of bed."

Ben was very much aware of the positive impression he was making. "I took care not only to be in *reality* industrious and frugal," he wrote, "but to avoid all *appearances* of the contrary." When he bought rolls of paper for his press, he made a show of personally carting the paper in a wheelbarrow down the street to his shop.

With energy to spare, Ben organized a club of bright young artisans and tradesmen who met every Friday evening to chat, laugh, drink, and sing, and, not the least, improve their minds. At every meeting they exchanged ideas and debated topics ranging from "What is happiness?" to "Why does condensation form on the outside of a mug of cold water in the summer?" They called themselves the Junto (meaning "conference"). During their discussions, Franklin, an engaging conversationalist when he cared to be, took pains not to dominate the discussion. Knowledge, he realized, "was obtained rather by the use of the ear than of the tongue." Not only that, but listening to what others had to say was the best way to win them over to his own point of view.

By now, Franklin was growing tired of his life as a freewheeling bachelor. At the age of twenty-four, "having turned my thoughts to marriage," he won the hand of Deborah Read, the girl he had been courting on and off since first coming to Philadelphia. "She proved a good and faithful helpmate," Franklin wrote, "assisted me much by attending the shop, we throve together, and have ever mutually endeavored to make each other happy."

Together Ben and Deborah raised Ben's son, William, born earlier to a mother Franklin never identified. Deborah gave birth to a boy, Francis, who died

Portrait of Deborah Franklin, attributed to Benjamin Wilson.

of smallpox at the age of four. Years later, the Franklins had a second child, a girl named Sarah, usually called Sally, who remained close to her father throughout his life.

Franklin's printing shop expanded to sell books and stationery, soaps made by Ben's Boston relatives, and ointments made by Deborah's mother, along with coffee, tea, chocolate, fish, and cheese. Deborah handled the bookkeeping and made clothes for her family, sewing by candlelight. A plain, practical, industrious woman, she called Franklin "Pappy." He called her "my dear child."

To keep his press busy, Franklin had purchased a weekly newspaper, *The Pennsylvania Gazette*, and turned it into the leading paper in Pennsylvania. Then he decided to publish an almanac. Almanacs were tremendously popular and profitable, since they had to be bought anew each year. Almost every colonial household had one. They were packed with useful features—the year's calendar, weather forecasts, the schedule of tides, times for the rising and setting of the sun and moon, when to plant each crop.

Franklin's version, called *Poor Richard's Almanack*, first published in 1733, offered all the usual features along with nuggets of personal advice and "many pleasant and Witty Verses, Jests, and Sayings," such as: "When you're good to others, you are best to yourself"; "Eat to please thyself, but dress to please others"; "God helps them that help themselves"; and the most famous of all, "Early to bed and early to rise makes a man healthy wealthy and wise."

What helped make Franklin wealthy was the publication of his almanac, which sold thousands of copies year after year.

As the prime mover of the Junto, Franklin rallied support for a variety of civic improvements. What "the good men may do sepa-

Franklin's print and bookshop. An early twentieth-century painting by Jean Leon Gerome Ferris.

Poor Richard, 1733.

AN

Almanack

For the Year of Chrift

1733,

Being the Firft after LEAP YEAR:

And makes fince the Creation	Years
By the Account of the Eastern *Greeks*	7241
By the Latin Church, when ☉ ent. ♈	6932
By the Computation of *W. W.*	5742
By the *Roman* Chronology	5682
By the *Jewish* Rabbies	5494

Wherein is contained

The Lunations, Eclipfes, Judgment of the Weather, Spring Tides, Planets Motions & mutual Afpects, Sun and Moon's Rifing and Setting, Length of Days, Time of High Water, Fairs, Courts, and obfervable Days.

Fitted to the Latitude of Forty Degrees, and a Meridian of Five Hours Weft from *London*, but may without fenfible Error, ferve all the adjacent Places, even from *Newfoundland to South-Carolina.*

By *RICHARD SAUNDERS*, Philom.

PHILADELPHIA:

Printed and fold by *B. FRANKLIN*, at the New Printing-Office near the Market.

The first edition of Poor Richard's Almanack, *1733.*

rately," he wrote, "is small compared with what they may do collectively." He suggested that his fellow Junto members pool their books to establish America's first lending library, the Library Company of Philadelphia, incorporated in 1731. Subscribers had the right to borrow books, most of which were eventually imported from London. The Library Company thrives today as an independent research library specializing in American history. Free and open to the public, it is one of the oldest cultural institutions in the United States.

During the next few years, Franklin and the Junto proposed and supervised the first plans to sweep and light Philadelphia's streets. They founded the city's first firefighting company, made up of thirty volunteers; the first hospital, open free of charge to the city's needy; and the first college, the Philadelphia Academy, which became the University of Pennsylvania. Since Franklin never had a chance to attend college, he made up for it by founding one.

He also founded the colonies' first learned society, the American Philosophical Society for Promoting Useful Knowledge. Members of this group were scientists, scholars, and artists living in the American colonies who shared their ideas and discoveries through correspondence. The society continues to flourish today, holding meetings twice a year in an old building next door to Philadelphia's Independence Hall.

Along with his civic-improvement projects, Franklin embarked on an ambitious campaign of self-improvement—his Moral Perfection Project. "I wished to live without committing any fault at any time," he recalled. "As I knew, or thought I knew, what was right and wrong, I did not see why I might not *always* do the one and avoid the other."

He made up a list of thirteen virtues that he thought desirable, such as *Frugality* ("Waste nothing"), *Industry* ("Be always employed in something useful"), and *Humility* ("Imitate Jesus and Socrates"). He kept a little notebook in which he recorded his daily shortcomings and faults. But mastering those faults was "a task more difficult" than he had expected. "While my attention was taken up in guarding against one fault, I was often surprised by another."

Franklin worked at his self-improvement plan "with occasional intermissions for some time. I was surprised to find myself so much fuller of faults than I had imagined, but I had the satisfaction of seeing them diminish." Eventually, a busy man of affairs, he tapered off and finally gave up his daily notations, "but I always carried my little book with me."

Meanwhile, his printing business prospered. He expanded, sponsoring printing shops far beyond Philadelphia in partnership with his employees. Franklin furnished the presses and equipment they needed in return for a share of their profits. Eventually he had an interest in more than two dozen printing shops scattered from New England to the Caribbean islands.

At home, his business was fueled by his friendships with Philadelphia's leading citizens. Appointed in 1736 as clerk of the Pennsylvania Assembly, a position he held for fifteen years, he became the colony's official printer, "which secured to me the business of printing the votes, laws, paper money, and other occasional jobs for the public, that on the whole were very profitable." A year later, he was also named Philadelphia postmaster, giving him a big advantage in the distribution of his newspaper and almanac.

By the time he was forty-two, Franklin was rich enough to retire. Freed from the need for money, he could exchange the leather apron of a workingman for the velvet coat of a gentleman. He looked forward to enjoying "what I look upon as a great happiness, leisure to read, study, make experiments, and converse at length with such ingenious and worthy men as are pleased to honor me with their friendship." He was already deeply engaged in the electrical experiments that would make him famous.

He retired from business, but not from printing. For the rest of his life, Franklin took pride in being a printer. Wherever he lived in Europe or America, he always had a press at his disposal. His last will and testament, written at the age of eighty-three, a year before his death, begins with the words, *"I Benjamin Franklin of Philadelphia, Printer…"*

The earliest portrait of Benjamin Franklin, painted by Robert Feke the year Franklin retired at forty-two.

Chapter Three

Snatching Lightning from the Sky

Franklin at work in his study.

Benjamin Franklin had been dreaming up experiments ever since he sent a kite aloft and let it pull him across a Boston pond. Some of his experiments had a practical purpose and resulted in useful inventions. Others were inspired by pure curiosity. Once his curiosity was aroused, he could not resist planning an experiment, and when luck was with him, he enjoyed the thrill of discovery.

In one early experiment, Franklin and a fellow Junto member tested the effects of heat on different colors. Which colors absorb, and which repel, the sun's rays? And what difference does it make? The two men placed cloth patches of different colors on a bed of snow. They calculated how much the sun heated each patch by measuring the melting snow under the patch. They found that dark colors absorb heat better than light ones.

Franklin put their findings to practical use, concluding that "black clothes are not so fit to wear in a hot sunny climate," that "soldiers and seamen who must march and labor in the sun should in the East or West

Indies have a uniform of white," and that the walls of fruit sheds should be painted black to absorb daytime heat and keep the shed warm through the night, "to preserve the fruit from frosts" and hasten ripening.

To investigate the causes of poor indoor heating, Franklin made a study of air currents and heat transfer. At the time, most homes were heated by wood fires blazing in open fireplaces. The problem was that much of the warm air went up the chimney, while smoke from the fire drifted out into the room. Franklin's experiments led to his invention of a new kind of wood-burning stove that could be built into a fireplace. Called the

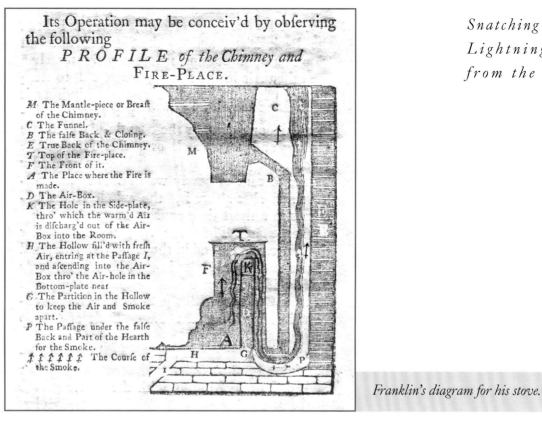

Franklin's diagram for his stove.

Pennsylvania fireplace (and known today as the Franklin stove), it was designed to radiate heat out into the room while sending smoke up the chimney.

Franklin refused to patent his stove. "As we enjoy great advantages from the inventions of others," he wrote, "we should be glad of an opportunity to serve others by any invention of ours, and this we should do freely and generously."

While *Poor Richard's Almanack* helped make Franklin rich, his experiments with electricity are what made him famous. In his day, knowledge of electricity remained about where it had been in ancient Greece. No one imagined that this mysterious force would one day be harnessed to create the world's most important source of light and power. Most people thought of electricity as a curious amusement, a source of amazing tricks performed by traveling showmen who called themselves "electricians."

Franklin attended one of those performances while visiting his family in Boston in 1743. The

An electrical experiment in France around 1755 demonstrates how the human body conducts electricity.

electrician's most spectacular stunt was to suspend a boy from the ceiling by silken cords while drawing "sparks, of fire" from his face and hands by rubbing his feet with a glass tube.

Franklin was fascinated. He wrote to a friend in London asking for more information about this "subject [that is] quite new to me." The friend sent him a long glass tube of the sort used by electricians to generate static electricity and create their effects, along with instructions for conducting electrical experiments. (Static electricity, the only kind of electricity known at the time, is what

produces a shock when you walk across a rug on a dry, cold day and touch a doorknob, or makes your hair stand on end when you pull off a cap on a winter day.)

"I eagerly seized the opportunity of repeating what I had seen at Boston," Franklin wrote, "and by much practice acquired great readiness in performing those also which we had an account of from England, adding a number of new ones.... My house was continually full for some time, with people who came to see these new wonders."

Franklin obtained one of the newly invented Leyden jars, which could capture and store electrical charges—"this miraculous bottle," he called it. Working by trial and error during the next five years, he explored what this "electric fluid" could and could not do. Eventually he was able to distinguish between *positive* and *negative* charges of electricity, between *conductors* and *nonconductors*—terms he created that are used today. He made history's first "electrical battery," another term he invented, and a "self-moving wheel," a small electric motor. And he discovered what he called "the wonderful effects of points": a sharply pointed metal rod would attract an electrical spark from a much greater distance than a blunt one.

"I was never before engaged in any study that so totally engrossed my attention and my time," Franklin told a friend. His experiments gave him and his Junto friends a chance to have some fun. He made a charged metal spider that jumped about like a real one, "appearing perfectly alive," and rigged a portrait of King George II to produce a shock when someone touched the monarch's golden crown.

For months he had "little leisure for anything else" other than his experiments. A couple of those experiments resulted in painful shocks, knocking him senseless. At first he could not think of any practical use for his findings. The only "use discovered of electricity," he wrote, was that "it may help to make a vain man humble."

Scientists in Europe had guessed that lightning was actually an electrical occurrence, but no one had tried to test this idea. Franklin made a list of the similarities between flashes of lightning and the "electric fluid" he had been experimenting with—swift motion, crooked direction, an explosive cracking sound, among others. He was convinced that lightning was not a supernatural phenomenon, as some people believed, but powerful electric sparks passing between clouds, or between clouds and the earth. "Since they agree in all the particulars wherein we can readily compare them," he wrote, "is it not probable they agree likewise in [both being electric]?"

He added: "Let the experiment be made."

Franklin's idea was to place a sentry box big enough to hold a man on top of a tower or steeple, with a tall, sharply pointed metal rod rising from the top of the box. The brave individual standing in the box during a thunderstorm would hold a looped wire by an insulated handle. Franklin had already discovered that electric sparks are attracted to pointed metal rods. If lightning struck the rod atop the sentry box and sparks flew from the bottom of the rod to the looped wire, it would prove that lightning and electricity are one and the same. Since Philadelphia had no high towers at the time, Franklin decided to wait and conduct his experiment from the steeple of Christ Church, which was still under construction.

Meanwhile, he had been describing his experiments in letters to friends in England. In 1751 the letters were published in a book titled *Experiments and Observations on Electricity, Made at Philadelphia in America,* which was translated into French, German, and Italian. On May 10, 1752, scientists in France, using a forty-foot-high iron lightning rod, successfully performed Franklin's experiment, drawing sparks from a passing storm cloud as Franklin had predicted. "Mr. Franklin's idea has ceased to be a conjecture," they reported. "Here it has been made a reality."

Before news of the French success could reach America, Franklin, waiting impatiently for the Christ Church steeple to be erected, came up with an entirely different way to conduct his lightning rod experiment. As a boy, he had used a kite to pull himself across a Boston pond. Now he thought of attaching a miniature lightning rod to a kite and sending it aloft during a thunderstorm.

He made a kite of silk rather than paper, since "silk is fitter to bear the wet and wind of a thunder gust without tearing." A twine string attached to the tail of the kite would conduct electricity, especially when wet. A large metal key tied to the end of the string at ground level would absorb an electric charge that ran down the string. To protect himself against a strong electrical jolt, Franklin tied a silk ribbon to the bottom of the string; if kept dry, the silk would insulate his hand from the wet string and the key.

Would the experiment work? Franklin, not yet aware of the success in France, wasn't sure. He decided to carry out his experiment in secret. With his son, William, at his

EXPERIMENTS

AND

OBSERVATIONS

O N

ELECTRICITY,

MADE AT

Philadelphia in *America,*

BY

Mr. BENJAMIN FRANKLIN,

AND

Communicated in several Letters to Mr. P. COLLINSON, of *London,* F. R. S.

LONDON:

Printed and sold by E. CAVE, at St. John's Gate. 1751.
(Price 2s. 6d.)

Franklin's electrical experiments were published in English, French, German, and Italian.

side, he walked out to a lonely field on a June day in 1752, waited for a summer thunderstorm, and let the silk kite fly.

Nothing happened at first. But then, as thunderheads scudded across the stormy sky and lightning flashed, Franklin pressed his knuckle against the key and felt an unmistakable electric shock, then several shocks more. "Let the reader judge the exquisite pleasure he must have felt at that moment," the British scientist Joseph Priestly wrote.

That settled it. Lightning and electricity were one and the same.

Franklin didn't know it yet, but his work had already caused a sensation in Europe. In quick succession, scientists had successfully repeated his lightning-rod experiment from lofty sentry boxes in France, England, and Germany. A Swedish scientist, not as fortunate, was electrocuted while carrying out the experiment.

King Louis XV of France sent "compliments to Mr. Franklin of Philadelphia for the useful discoveries in electricity and application of the pointed rods to prevent the terrible effects of thunderstorms." People had always been defenseless against the deadly effect of lightning striking houses and churches. Now, buildings of any kind could be protected by Franklin's tall, pointed lightning rods, which attracted bolts of lightning and sent them down a wire outside the building and harmlessly into the ground.

Franklin did not fail to pro-

Franklin conducted his kite experiment in June, 1752, with the help of his son, William, who was twenty-two at the time, unlike the boy depicted in this popular Currier and Ives print published in 1895.

PUBLISHED BY CURRIER & IVES   Copyright, 1876 by Currier & Ives, New York.   125 NASSAU ST. NEW YORK

FRANKLIN'S EXPERIMENT, JUNE 1752.
Demonstrating the identity of Lightning and Electricity, from which he invented the Lightning Rod.

mote the practical benefits of his discovery. The new edition of *Poor Richard's Almanack* included an account of "how to secure houses, etc., from lightning." Franklin installed a lightning rod atop his own house, hooked up to an ingenious device that rang a bell outside his bedroom door when a storm approached. Before long, houses all over the colonies were protected by lightning rods on the roofs and heated by Franklin stoves in their sitting rooms.

Harvard and Yale universities awarded Franklin honorary degrees. "Thus, without studying in any college, I came to partake of these honors," he wrote. He became the first person outside Great Britain to be awarded the Royal Society's gold Copely Medal, and later, to Franklin's delight, to be elected a member of that British society. In Germany, the great philosopher Immanuel Kant compared Franklin to the mythological Greek Titan Prometheus, who stole fire from the heavens and gave it to humanity.

Much to his surprise, Ben Franklin had become the world's most famous American. He admitted cheerfully that he enjoyed his international reputation, even though, he told a friend, "we are generally hypocrites in that respect, and pretend to disregard praise."

One of Franklin's first lightning rods was installed on the house of his close friend, artist Benjamin West.

Chapter Four

Following the Example
of the Iroquois

When Franklin retired, he expected to enjoy "leisure during the rest of my life, for [scientific] studies and amusements." But he found that his time was no longer his own. He had become a public figure, and "the public, now considering me as a man of leisure, laid hold of me for their purposes."

In quick succession, "every part of our civil government...imposed some duty on me." He was elected to the Philadelphia City Council, appointed a justice of the peace, named a city alderman, and finally, in 1751, elected to a seat in the Pennsylvania Assembly, where he had worked as clerk for the past fifteen years.

"My ambition was...flattered by all these promotions," he confessed. "It certainly was. For considering my low beginning they were great things to me. And they were still more pleasing, as being so many spontaneous testimonies of the public's good opinion, and by me entirely unsolicited."

Franklin would win reelection to the assembly every year for the next ten years. At the same time, he took on a new responsibility. The British government appointed him deputy postmaster general for the colonies, the top post-office job in America. Applying everything he had learned as Philadelphia's postmaster, he set in motion a sweeping overhaul of postal delivery. He introduced night postal riders—a forerunner of the pony express—cutting to a single day the delivery time of a letter between Philadelphia and New York. A correspondent in Philadelphia could post a letter to New York one day and receive a reply the next—a delivery time that has not been surpassed even today. Franklin also introduced America's first home-delivery system. Letters that weren't picked

Postmaster General Benjamin Franklin hands mail to a post rider in this 1945 painting by Franklin J. Reilly.

up the day they arrived at the post office were delivered the next day by the "penny postman" for an extra fee.

While Franklin was improving the postal service, fighting was breaking out along America's western frontier. England and France had been skirmishing for years to determine which nation would rule North America. In 1754, French troops with their Indian allies swept down from Canada, aiming to grab control of the Ohio River valley. Their goal was to build a series of forts along the Ohio River, securing French possession of a vast territory stretching from Canada to Louisiana.

The French forts were seen as a threat to England's colonies along the Atlantic coast. French troops and fur traders were moving aggressively into the backcountry of New York, Pennsylvania, and Virginia, planting the French flag in the colonies' backyards. That summer, tensions erupted into the full-scale conflict that the colonists, who remained loyal to England, called the French and Indian War.

As the fighting escalated, a conference was arranged in Albany, New York, between the colonists and their chief Indian allies, the powerful Iroquois confederacy of six nations—Mohawks, Oneidas, Senecas, Cayugas, Tuscaroras, and Onondagas—who lived along the lakes just south of Canada. Franklin attended as a delegate from Pennsylvania. The conference had two objectives: to renew the colonists' alliance with the Iroquois, and to create a plan by which the individual colonies would band together and unite for their common defense against the French.

The colonies were independent of one another, each with its own government, and they did not

King Philip (Metacomet), sachem of the Massachusetts Wampanoags, signs a treaty with English settlers in 1671. Five years later, Philip was killed in a war with the colonists, a conflict that brought ruin to his tribe. During the 1700s, the Iroquois of New York also signed treaties with English settlers and sided with them against the French in the French and Indian War.

always cooperate. Only seven of England's thirteen American colonies attended the Albany Conference. The others didn't bother to send delegates. Franklin was convinced that if the colonists were to defend themselves, they would have to agree on some sort of union.

He pointed to the Iroquois confederacy as an example of cooperation that should shame those colonists who placed their local interests ahead of the common welfare. "It would be a very strange thing," he wrote, "if six nations of [the Iroquois] should be capable of forming a scheme for such a union… [that] has subsisted for ages, and appears indissoluble; and yet that a like union should be impracticable for ten or a dozen English colonies, to whom it is more necessary, and must be more advantageous."

Before traveling to the Albany Congress, Franklin wrote an editorial for his newspaper, *The Pennsylvania Gazette*, on the need for unity among the colonies. The French believed that they could take over the Ohio valley, he wrote, because of "the disunited states of the British colonies, and the extreme difficulty of bringing so many different governments and assemblies to agree in any speedy and effectual measures for our common defense." So long as the colonies remained disunited, Franklin argued, the French "could take an easy possession of such parts of the British territory as they find most convenient for them."

Accompanying the editorial was a drawing of a snake's body cut into pieces labeled with the initials of England's American colonies. Below the drawing was the motto "Join, or Die." This was another first for Franklin—the first original political cartoon printed in America.

Franklin arrived in Albany with a proposal called "Short Hints towards a Scheme for Uniting the Northern Colonies." Agreeing

In America's earliest political cartoon, Franklin warned the colonists to unite against the French and their Indian allies. The parts of the segmented snake are labeled for South Carolina, North Carolina, Virginia, Maryland, Pennsylvania, New Jersey, New York, and New England (which was actually four colonies). Delaware and Maryland are missing.

that some kind of colonial union was necessary, the delegates assigned a committee to report on Franklin's plan. Meanwhile the Iroquois arrived, led by the renowned Mohawk chief Tiyanoga, also known as Hendrick Peters. A tall, commanding figure in his seventies, Tiyanoga was described at the time as "singularly impressive . . . with an air of majesty . . . as if born to control other men." From the left side of his mouth, a tomahawk scar ran across his cheek—a warrior's badge of courage.

He strode forward to address the assembly. "Look about your country and see, you have no fortifications about you," he warned. " 'Tis but one step from Canada hither, and the French may easily come and turn you out of doors. Brethren! You desire us to speak from the bottom of our hearts, and we shall do it. . . . Look at the French! They are men, they are fortifying everywhere. But—we are ashamed to say it—you are all like women, bare and open without any fortifications."

After a week of speeches and an exchange of gifts, the colonists and the Iroquois "solemnly renewed" their alliance. The American delegates then voted to adopt a unification plan based on Franklin's proposal—a national congress made up of representatives from all the colonies, with a president appointed by the British king. The proposed congress would deal with colonial defense and relations with the Indian Nations, while each colony would keep its own constitution and government.

But the Albany Plan of Union was too far ahead of its time. When the delegates returned home, every colonial assembly, unwilling to give up its powers, rejected the plan. It was turned down as well by the British government. British officials worried that if the colonies banded together, they might demand a greater degree of independence from England.

That wasn't what Franklin had in mind. Like most American colonists at the time, he considered himself a loyal British subject. In his view, a union of the colonies would be a jewel in the British Empire's crown. Franklin wanted the people of Great Britain and the American colonies to

Hendrick Peters (Tiyanoga), the great sachem of the Mohawks. A 1755 engraving.

William Penn signs a treaty with Tamanend and other Delaware chiefs, founding the province of Pennsylvania in 1681. A 1775 engraving after a painting by Benjamin West.

WILLIAM PENN's Treaty with the INDIANS, when he founded the PROVINCE of PENSYLVANIA in NORTH AMERICA 1681.

be treated as equals, to "consider themselves not as belonging to different communities with different interests, but to one community with one interest."

In coming years, the Albany Plan would become a model for cooperative action by the colonies. "I am still of the opinion that it would have been happy for both sides…if it had been adopted," Franklin wrote. "But such mistakes are not new; history is full of the errors of states and princes."

Back in Philadelphia, the big issue facing the Pennsylvania Assembly was a question of fair and equal taxation. Pennsylvania, founded in 1681 by William Penn under a charter from the British king, was still governed by the powerful Penn family, which owned most of the unsettled land. Like other colonies, Pennsylvania had to raise money for its own defense, so the assembly passed a bill taxing all property in the colony. But the Penns opposed any measure that would subject their own land to taxes. They insisted that their property was exempt from taxation.

Angry messages were exchanged between the elected assembly and the Penn-appointed governor. "Our answers as well as his messages were often tart, and sometimes indecently abusive," Franklin told a friend. The Penns were subjects of the king just as much as he was. He was outraged at their refusal to pay taxes on their lands like everyone else.

Thomas Penn, the son of William Penn, ruled the colony from London, where he now lived. He called Franklin "a dangerous man and I should be very glad [if] he inhabited any other country."

As the dispute heated up, the Pennsylvania Assembly voted to send a mission to England to argue its case with the Penn family, and if that failed, with the British government. Franklin, now fifty-one, was chosen as the assembly's agent. He looked forward to taking on this new role as a diplomat.

William Penn.

Richard Peters, the Penn family's private secretary, suspected that Franklin's real purpose was to persuade the British Parliament to take control of Pennsylvania away from the Penns. "B.F.'s view is to effect a change of government," Peters warned, "and considering the popularity of his character and the reputation gained by his electrical discoveries, which will introduce him into all sorts of company, he may prove a dangerous enemy."

"Mr. Franklin's popularity is nothing here," replied Thomas Penn from his London estate. "He will be looked upon very coldly by great people."

Franklin decided to take his son, William, now twenty-seven, with him to London. His wife, Deborah, and their fourteen-year-old daughter, Sally, would remain behind. Deborah, a homebody, feared the lengthy ocean crossing. And she wasn't anxious to join her husband in the sophisticated, fashionable world of the London aristocracy.

Chapter Five

Dr. Fatsides in the Mother Country

Dr. Franklin, a.k.a. "Dr. Fatsides." Portrait by an unidentified artist, after Mason Chamberlain.

"A fat old fellow," as he described himself, Franklin returned to London thirty-three years after his first visit there as an ambitious teenage printer. He had come to argue the Pennsylvania Assembly's side in its dispute with the Penn family.

He rented four furnished rooms in the home of Margaret Stevenson, an accommodating widow who lived with her lively eighteen-year-old daughter, Polly. William enrolled in law school and served as his father's secretary. Mrs. Stevenson and Polly doted on the two Americans, catering to their needs, caring for Franklin when he was ill, providing a comforting home away from home.

Franklin and his son took careful note of the latest London fashions. Their earliest expenditures included new shoes and wigs, fine linen to be made into shirts, silver shoe and knee buckles, and copies of *The Gentleman's Magazine.* Franklin ordered new spectacles for himself and bought a watch at auction. And he hired his own coach and driver for twelve guineas a month.

London, the biggest city in Europe, attracted talented and ambitious people from all over the British Empire. They gathered to meet and talk in hundreds of clubs, coffeehouses, taverns, and theaters. "Early to bed and early to rise" may have been a sensible rule back home in Philadelphia,

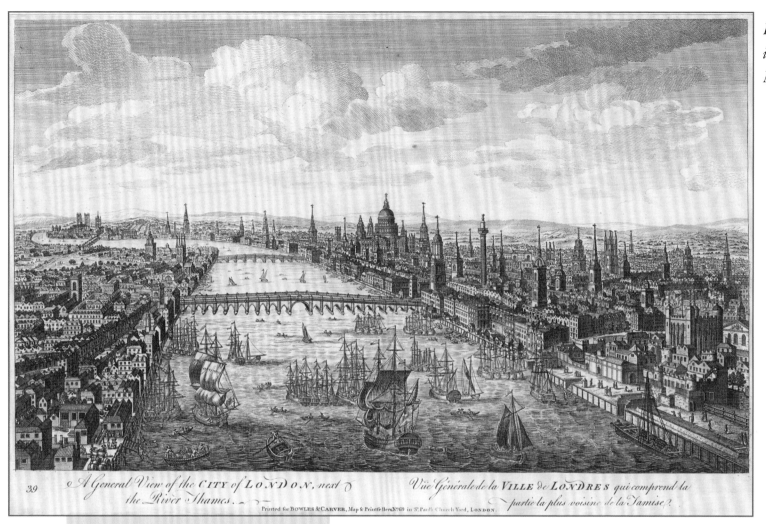

London and the River Thames around 1760.

but in London people liked to stay up late. Walking around his neighborhood early one morning, Franklin noted, "There was not one shop open though it had been daylight and the sun up above three hours. The inhabitants of London [choose] voluntarily to live much by candlelight and sleep by sunshine."

With his expansive good fellowship and his fame, Franklin was welcomed into several London

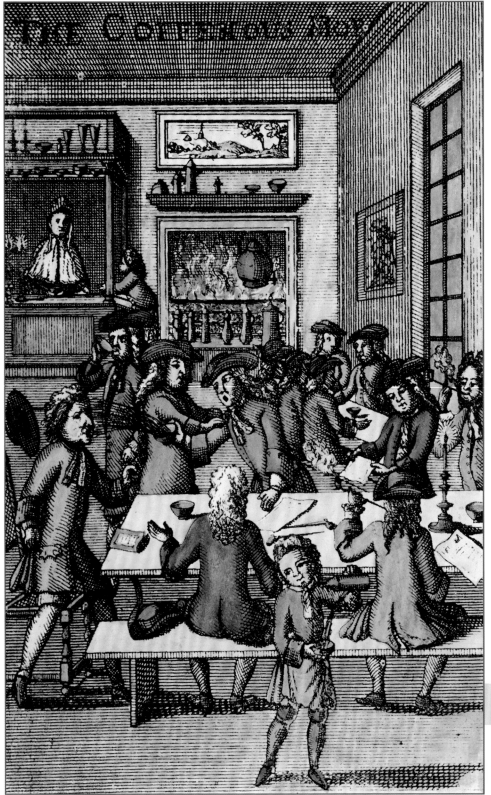

Socializing in a London coffeehouse.

clubs. He met writers, artists, and scientists who were eager to exchange ideas with him, and he entertained his friends at dinner parties in his rooms. "Conversation," he wrote, "warms the mind."

Cambridge University invited him to demonstrate his electricity experiments. He and William "were present at all the ceremonies, dined every day in their halls," he wrote to Deborah. "My vanity was not a little gratified by the particular regard showed [me] by the chancellor and vice-chancellor of the university." Oxford University and Scotland's University of St. Andrews awarded him honorary doctoral degrees. "Dr. Franklin looks heartier than I ever knew him in America," reported an American friend visiting London.

Franklin usually began his day with an hourlong morning "air bath." He would fling open the windows, "sit in my chamber without any clothes whatsoever," and let the warm or cold air, depending on the season, bathe his portly body. He had long since lost the taut swimmer's physique of his youth and had put on weight, considered in those days a mark of prosperity. Some of his English friends, noting his "enormous size," his "broad-built bulk," called him "Dr. Fatsides," an affectionate nickname he cheerfully adopted.

✳　✳　✳

As the special agent, or lobbyist, for Pennsylvania, Franklin's mission was to resolve the dispute between the Pennsylvania Assembly and the Penn family, the proprietors of the colony.

The Penns continued to claim that their lands were exempt from taxes. Another disagreement concerned the powers of the colonial governor, appointed by the Penns, versus the powers of the assembly, elected by the voters. Who had the right to pass and approve the colony's laws—the assembly, as Franklin believed, or the governor, as the Penns insisted?

Franklin's negotiations with Thomas Penn turned out to be far more heated than he had expected. The two men disagreed from the start. Penn complained that Franklin, that "dangerous man," had failed to pay him the proper respect. Franklin expressed "a more thorough contempt for him than I have ever before felt for any man living—a contempt that I cannot express in words, but I believe my countenance expressed it strongly." Richard Peters, the Penns' secretary, had noted that when angry, Franklin's "face turns white as the driven snow with the extremes of wrath."

Penn refused to meet with Franklin again. He turned the matter over to his lawyers. The Penns were skilled politicians with connections to all the right people, and the negotiations seemed to drag on endlessly. Franklin learned what it was like to be snubbed, to cool his heels in the waiting rooms of the high and mighty.

Instead of the brief stay he had expected, Franklin was to spend more than five years in England. While he waited for word from Penn's lawyers, he enjoyed his expanding circle of friends in London and his travels with William through England and Scotland. "The regard and friendship I meet with from persons of worth, and the conversation of ingenious men, gave me no small pleasure," he told Deborah.

He found time to invent a three-wheeled clock that showed the seconds as well as the hours and minutes, and a new musical instrument, the glass "armonica." Then as now, dinner guests sometimes amused themselves by moving a wet finger around the rim of a glass and producing a ringing tone. Franklin had attended a London concert of music performed on wine glasses. He carried this idea a step further by rigging a kind of spinning wheel with a foot pedal and attaching thirty-seven glass bowls of differing sizes. By spinning the wheel and pressing his wet fingers on the glass, he was able to produce a variety of musical tones.

"It is an instrument that seems particularly adapted to Italian music," he wrote to a friend in Italy, "especially of the soft and plaintive kind." The armonica became a popular musical

THOMAS PENN.
Colonial Governor of Penn.ª

Thomas Penn, royal governor of Pennsylvania. He called Franklin "a dangerous man."

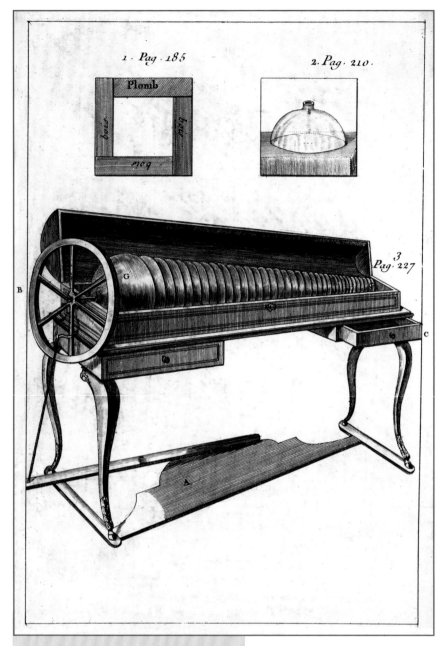

Franklin's musical instrument, the glass armonica, invented in 1762.

instrument at weddings. Mozart and Beethoven wrote pieces for it. And Marie Antoinette took lessons on it.

Franklin had written to Deborah that negotiations with the Penns would require "both time and patience." As his months in England turned into years, he sent crates of gifts home to his wife and daughter—fine silver and china, French silk blankets, "a crimson satin cloak for you [Deborah], the newest fashion, and the black silk [one] for Sally." One gift, "a large fine jug for beer, to stand in the cooler," reminded him, he hinted, of his absent wife. "I fell in love with it at first sight, for I thought it looked like a fat jolly dame, clean and tidy, with a neat blue and white calico gown on, good-natured and lovely, and put me in mind of—somebody." By comparing his wife to a shapely beer jug, Franklin was actually praising Deborah. In colonial America, an ample figure was seen as a sign of robust good health, and in women, an expression of beauty

A friend in Philadelphia wrote that Deborah and Sally endured Franklin's "long absence with a more resigned and Christian spirit than could be expected." Many Philadelphians, the friend added, were wondering when Franklin would return home.

Like most colonists in America, Franklin looked upon England as the mother country. He was tempted, he admitted, to settle permanently in England. With William, he visited cousins he had never met in Northamptonshire, where Franklin's father had lived before emigrating to America. And he looked up Deborah's kinfolk in Birmingham. "They are industrious, ingenious, hard-working people," he reported to his wife, "and think themselves vastly happy that they live in dear old England."

In an article written for a London newspaper, Franklin expressed his "respect for the mother country, and admiration of everything that is British." And while he continued to hope that the American colonies would unite, he was convinced that they would remain a loyal part of the British Empire, "which protects and encourages them, with which they have so many connections and ties of blood, interest, and affection."

At the time, Franklin could not foresee the troubles that lay ahead. So long as Britain avoided "tyranny and oppression," he argued, the colonies would never rebel. United, they would be part of a greater British Empire. "I have long been of [the] opinion that the foundations of the future grandeur and stability of the British Empire lie in America," he told a friend.

The Penns eventually agreed to pay limited taxes on their lands. But they continued to insist that they alone, through instructions to their governors, had the power to make the colony's laws. The elected assembly could offer "advice and consent," but nothing more. Franklin had won a partial victory. While it fell short of what he had hoped for, he had, during his stay in England, made lasting friendships with all sorts of people, winning their affection and esteem. Through the influence of one friend, William was appointed royal governor of New Jersey.

It was time to return home, to "the happy society of my friends and family in Philadelphia." But he fully expected to return to England. "I shall probably...settle here forever," he told a friend on the eve of his departure. "Nothing will prevent it if I can, as I hope I can, prevail with Mrs. F. to accompany me."

✳ ✳ ✳

Back in Philadelphia, the streets seemed "thinner of people, owing perhaps to my being so long accustomed to the bustling crowded streets of London." Franklin's house, however, was filled with friends welcoming him back, "a succession of them from morning to night ever since my arrival."

Franklin and his daughter, Sally, delighted in entertaining their guests.

Franklin's daughter, Sarah Franklin Bache, known as "Sally." Portrait by John Hoppner.

"She sings the songs to her harpsichord, and I play some of the softest tunes on my armonica, with which entertainment the people here are quite charmed, and conceive the Scottish tunes to be the finest in the world."

As soon as he returned, Franklin took his seat in the Pennsylvania Assembly. The voters had continued to reelect him every year while he was living in London. And he still held his appointment as deputy postmaster, so he set off on a postal inspection tour that took him from Virginia to New Hampshire, traveling some 1,600 miles on horseback and by carriage. Twice he suffered falls from his horse, dislocating his shoulder, a painful injury that took weeks to heal. "I am not yet able to travel rough roads," he complained. "I can neither hold reins nor whip with my right hand till it grows stronger."

He was scarcely back from his postal inspections when troubles erupted on Pennsylvania's western frontier. Angry at Indian raids, a mob of settlers had slaughtered at least twenty innocent Indian men, women, and children. Franklin assailed the attacks in an emotional pamphlet titled *A Narrative of the Late Massacres.* "Do we come to America to learn and practice the manners of *barbarians*?" he demanded. "If an Indian injured me, does it follow that I may revenge that injury on all Indians? . . . The only crime of the poor [victims] seems to have been, that they had a reddish-brown skin, and black hair."

John Penn, who succeeded his brother as Pennsylvania's royal governor. He called on Franklin to help put down an uprising by frontier settlers.

When hundreds of armed frontiersmen threatened to march on Philadelphia and wipe out the Indians who had fled to the city for safety, Pennsylvania's new governor, John Penn, called on Franklin to help put down the uprising. The governor "did me the honor, upon an alarm, to run to my house at midnight, with his counselors at his heels, for advice, and made it his headquarters for some time." Franklin joined a delegation of city leaders who met with the rioters and persuaded them to return home. "The fighting face we put on and the reasoning we used with the insurgents...turned them back and restored quiet to the city," he wrote.

The governor and the assembly were still at odds over who had the power to pass laws and levy taxes. Elected as speaker of the assembly, Franklin led a campaign to revoke William Penn's charter and make Pennsylvania a royal colony under the king's protection.

The next election was the most bitter ever fought in the colony. Franklin was accused, falsely, of stealing his electricity experiments from other scientists, buying his honorary degrees, and seeking a royal governorship for himself. The same governor who had run to him for help now assailed him as a "villain" with a "black heart." Franklin, in turn, charged that the Penns had acted in ways that were "tyrannical and inhuman." "All regard for [the governor] in the Assembly is lost," he wrote. "All hopes of happiness under a proprietary government are at an end."

When the votes were counted, Franklin lost his seat in the assembly—a defeat that stunned him. He had misjudged the feelings of many of his fellow colonists. His supporters, however, had kept control of the assembly. They voted to send Franklin back to England to represent the colonists' interests at the king's court and in the halls of Parliament.

Once again Franklin wanted Deborah to accompany him, and again she refused to set foot on an oceangoing ship. When Franklin sailed for England, Deborah settled into the fine new house they had just built, just steps from where she had first spotted Ben as a runaway apprentice.

Hundreds of cheering supporters saw Franklin off. He didn't know how long he would be away this time, and at fifty-six he felt he was getting on. "I am now to take leave (perhaps a last leave) of the country I love and in which I have spent the greatest part of my life," he said. "I wish every kind of prosperity to my friends, and I forgive my enemies."

Chapter Six

Becoming a Rebel

Tax stamps such as these had to be pasted on printed matter of every kind.

By Christmas of 1764, Franklin was back in London, comfortably settled in his old lodgings with Mrs. Stevenson and surrounded by friends delighted to see him again. England had a new king, George III, "the very best [ruler] in the world and the most amiable," according to Franklin. He believed that the young monarch would be sympathetic to the colonists' interests.

"A few months, I hope," he wrote to Deborah, "will finish affairs here to my wish, and bring me [back] to that retirement and repose with my little family." But instead of months, unexpected events were to keep him in England for the next ten years. Deborah stayed home in Philadelphia. She would never see her husband again.

Franklin had barely settled down when troubles broke out back home. The British Parliament had passed the Stamp Act, slapping an unpopular new tax on the Americans and throwing the colonies into turmoil. The colonists would now have to buy British tax stamps to paste on all printed matter issued in America—everything from newspapers and pamphlets to diplomas, marriage licenses, and wills.

The colonists did not object to paying taxes. But they insisted that *any* tax imposed by the distant British Parliament, a legislature in which they were not represented, was a violation of their rights. No one, they argued, had a right to tax them except their own elected representatives.

No taxation without representation became a battle cry that swept through the colonies. So strong was opposition to the stamp tax that riots broke out in town after town. Demonstrators threatened to seize and destroy the hated tax stamps, to demolish the offices where they were to be issued, and

Angry Bostonians reading the Stamp Act.

to tar and feather the tax collectors. On the day the Stamp Act was to take effect, not a single tax collector was in business anywhere in America.

In London, Franklin bent his efforts to getting the Stamp Act repealed. He was busy at all hours buttonholing members of Parliament, "informing, explaining, consulting, disputing, in a continual hurry from morning to night." He warned British officials that enforcing the Stamp Act would create "a deep-seated aversion between the two countries, laying the foundations of a future total separation." And he bombarded the British newspapers with articles written under a parade of pen names, arguing that his countrymen would never accept the hated stamp tax.

So Franklin was well prepared when he was summoned to appear before the British House of Commons and explain American opposition to the tax. Dressed plainly, his manner calm, his face composed, he told the lawmakers that before the Stamp Act, the colonists' loyalty to England was unquestioned. "They were governed…at the expense only of a little pen, ink and paper," he said.

*Franklin testifies before the House of Commons, 1766. An
early twentieth-century painting by Charles E. Mills.*

"They were led by a thread. They had not only a respect, but an affection, for Great Britain." But those warm feelings had been "very much altered" by the Stamp Act. Parliament had no right to impose a tax on the colonies, Franklin declared, "as we are not represented there."

Would the Americans agree to a compromise? he was asked. They would not, he replied, as the right to tax was a matter of principle. It was the colonists' right as British subjects to vote on their own taxes in their own legislative assemblies.

Would the Americans submit under the threat of military force? "I do not see how a military force can be applied to that purpose," Franklin answered. "[Soldiers] cannot force a man to take stamps who chooses to do without them. They will not find a rebellion; [but] they may indeed make one."

In all, Franklin answered 174 questions. He was on his feet for almost four hours. His calm and forthright testimony helped convince the lawmakers to repeal the Stamp Act. While some forty other persons were called to testify, many Americans gave Franklin credit for bringing about the repeal all by himself.

Franklin was pleased. He was now recognized in England as America's leading spokes-

man. Besides representing Pennsylvania, he was appointed agent for Georgia, New Jersey, and Massachusetts as well. He concentrated his efforts on restoring harmony and goodwill between Britain and the still-loyal American colonies.

"Being born and bred in one of the countries and having lived long and made many agreeable connections in the other, I wish all prosperity to both," he said.

✳　✳　✳

As a break from politics, Franklin advised friends on their smoky chimneys, had lightning rods installed atop St. Paul's Cathedral, and designed a system of hot-water pipes to help keep the House of Commons warm. He traveled to Scotland and Ireland, and across the English Channel to Holland and France. He started to write his autobiography. And he kept up a busy social life. "My company [is] so much desired," he wrote to William, "that I seldom dine at home in winter, and could spend the whole summer in the country houses of inviting friends, if I chose it."

But Franklin's optimism didn't last. King George and his ministers were determined to show that Britain still had the right to tax the colonies at any time. They pressured Parliament to pass the Townshend Acts, imposing taxes in the form of import duties on certain British goods shipped to America—paper, paint, glass, lead, and tea. The colonists demanded repeal of these new taxes. And they organized a boycott of all British goods, taxed or not. In London, Franklin warned that the king's misguided ministers were likely "to convert millions of…loyal subjects into rebels for the sake of establishing a newly claimed power in Parliament to tax a distant people."

British merchants complained that they were being ruined by the American boycott. So Parliament backed down again and repealed all the new taxes, except for one—a three-pennies-per-pound tax on tea, America's favorite beverage. The tea tax didn't amount to much, but the colonists refused to pay it. In place of tea shipped from England, they drank tea made from local herbs, or tea smuggled from Holland.

Franklin still hoped for reconciliation. To express his views without stirring up more trouble, he wrote anonymous satires for the British papers, poking fun at Britain's treatment of America. One was titled "Rules by Which a Great Empire May be Reduced to a Small One." "A great empire," Franklin wrote, "like a great cake, is most easily diminished at the edges."

The Boston Tea Party, December 16, 1773. An 1892 illustration by Howard Pyle.

Determined to break the boycott, England shipped large quantities of low-cost tea to the colonies, hoping to tempt the Americans to buy the bargain tea and pay the tax. That's when the Sons of Liberty, a band of Boston patriots, carried out a defiant act of protest, a dramatic deed that would set the colonies on the road to revolution. Disguised as Mohawk Indians, they boarded three tea ships tied up in Boston Harbor, dumped 342 chests of tea into the sea, and marched away to the music of a fife.

When news of the Boston Tea Party reached London, Franklin was singled out as a convenient scapegoat—a prominent American close at hand who could be blamed for England's mounting troubles in the unruly colonies. He was summoned to appear before the government's Privy Council in a famous room known as the Cockpit, where cockfights had been held during the reign of King Henry VIII. On January 29, 1774, the Cockpit was packed with council members and with scores of curious spectators, all eager to see how the celebrated Dr. Franklin would defend himself. "All the courtiers were invited," Franklin said, "as to an entertainment."

For almost an hour, the government prosecutor heaped abuse on Franklin. He was denounced as "the true incendiary" whose followers "have been inflaming the whole province [of Massachusetts] against His Majesty's government." He was a troublemaker who had "forfeited all the respect of societies and men."

Franklin said not a word in reply. Throughout the prosecutor's tirade, as the crowd cheered and laughed and jeered, he stood silently at the edge of the room, his face frozen, determined not to reveal the slightest hint of emotion. "The Doctor...stood conspicuously erect, without the smallest movement of any part of his body," a spectator reported. "The muscles of his face had been previously composed as to afford a tranquil, placid expression...and he did not suffer the slightest alteration of it to appear."

When the session ended, Franklin walked out calmly, his expression still unruffled. But his hopes for reconciliation between Great Britain and America had been shaken. And his personal resentment at being attacked so brutally can only be imagined. According to one story, he took the prosecutor by the arm as they left the Cockpit and whispered in his ear, "I will make your master a *little king* for this."

The next day, the British government fired Franklin from his position as deputy postmaster general for North America. For a time, he feared that his private papers might be confiscated.

Throughout this ordeal, his English friends stood by him. "Be assured," he told one of them, "that I have done nothing unjustified, nothing but what is consistent with the man of honor and with my duty to my king and country. I do not find that I have lost a single friend on the occasion. All have visited me repeatedly with affectionate assurances of their unaltered respect and affection."

As far as the British government was concerned, Franklin was now a political outcast. "I have seen no [government] minister since January," he wrote to his sister in September 1774, "nor had

Franklin stands silently as he is denounced in London's Cockpit, 1774. A nineteenth-century painting by Christian Schussele.

*King George III of Great Britain. He
was in no mood to compromise.*

the least communication with them." His wife and son were pleading with him to return to Phila-delphia. Even so, with no official business to conduct, he hung on in London, still hoping he could act as a mediator and make one last effort to save the Empire.

But King George and his ministers were in no mood to compromise. They prodded Parliament to pass a series of harsh laws, which the colonists called the "Intolerable Acts." Massachusetts was placed under strict military rule; town meetings, by which the colonists governed themselves, were curtailed; and Boston Harbor was closed to all shipping until the colonists paid for the ruined tea. "We must control them or submit to them," declared Frederick, Lord North, the king's prime minister.

The Intolerable Acts, meant to bring the rebellious colonists to their knees, instead inspired greater resistance. "Every act of oppression will...hasten [the colonies'] final revolt," Franklin predicted. The British writer Edmund Burke urged Parliament to "reflect on how you are to gov-ern [those] who think they ought to be free and think they are not." He warned the lawmakers that they might soon be "wading up to your eyes in blood."

In September 1774, every colony except Georgia sent delegates to the First Continental Congress in Philadelphia. As yet, few delegates were willing to speak openly about rebellion. Most of them hoped for a peaceful compromise that would guarantee the colonists' rights and liberties, yet allow them to remain within the British Empire. After seven weeks of debate, the delegates denounced British interference in colonial affairs, pledged their support to Massachusetts, and demanded that Parliament repeal all laws that restricted their liberties.

With other Americans in London, Franklin protested the Intolerable Acts and warned they could lead to war. His friends now urged him to leave England, but he felt that he still had some influence. He stayed on, waiting to learn what action the Continental Congress in Philadelphia would take.

"If by some accident the [British] troops and people of New England should come to blows, I should probably be [arrested]," he told an American friend. It was a risk he was willing to take. "The worst which can happen to me would be imprisonment on suspicion, though that is a thing I should desire to avoid, as it may be expensive...as well as dangerous to my health."

By early 1775, Franklin had given up all hope for a resolution of the crisis. King George had refused to accept a respectful petition from the Continental Congress, and the king's ministers had rejected any talk of a negotiated settlement. Parliament had declared the colony of Massachusetts in a state of rebellion.

In the midst of these troubles, Franklin received a sorrowful letter from his son, written weeks earlier in Philadelphia. "I came here on Thursday last to attend the funeral of my poor old mother," William informed him. Deborah had died after a lingering illness, without Franklin's presence or knowledge. William had made his way

Carpenter's Hall in Philadelphia, site of the First Continental Congress.

through a snowstorm to reach the graveyard in time for the funeral. He described his last visit with Deborah: "She told me that she never expected to see you again unless you returned this winter."

They had been married for forty-four years. Jolly, jug-shaped Deborah, as Franklin had so fondly imagined her, had devoted herself to Franklin's comfort and welfare at home and during his long absences in England. "It seems but the other day since you and I were ranked among the boys and girls, so swiftly does time fly," Franklin had written to her two years earlier. "We have, however, great reason to be thankful that so much of our lives has passed so happily."

William again urged his father to leave England. "You are looked upon with an evil eye in that country, and are in no small danger of being brought into trouble for your political conduct. You had certainly better return while you are able to bear the fatigues of the voyage to a country where the people revere you. I hope to see you... and that you will spend some time with me."

Franklin finally agreed that it was time to return to America. Despite his efforts, the empire he had once wanted to save was being "destroyed by the mangling hands of a few blundering [government] ministers."

The American colonies were heading toward rebellion, and Benjamin Franklin was ready to join them.

This political cartoon, published in England in 1779, shows a horse, "America," throwing its rider, King George III.

Chapter Seven

Declaring Independence

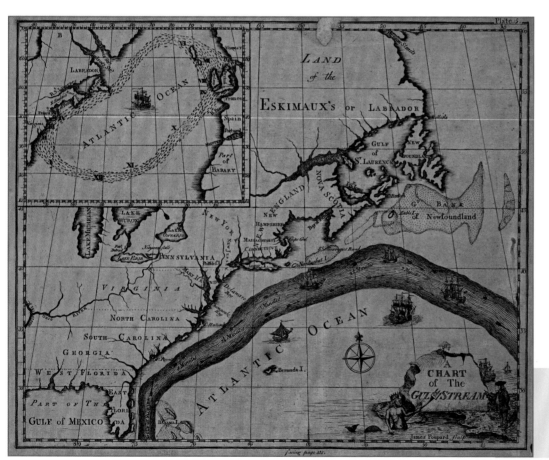

Franklin sailed back to America with his fifteen-year-old grandson Temple, William's son, who had been going to school in London. Just as William had helped with his father's kite-flying experiment, Temple now helped as his grandfather charted the course of the Gulf Stream, the warm ocean current that flows from the tip of Florida across the Atlantic to the coast of northern Europe.

Several times a day during their six-week voyage, Franklin and Temple lowered a homemade thermometer into the sea and recorded the water temperature on a chart. They noted that the water of the Gulf Stream, besides being warmer than the surrounding ocean, had a different color and contained more of what the sailors called "gulf weed." By catching a ride

On his sailings across the Atlantic, Franklin charted the course of the Gulf Stream. This map, based on his notes, was the first of its kind.

on this swift, powerful current, ships sailing from America to Europe could make faster time, while ships sailing to America could shorten the voyage by avoiding the current rather than running against it. Franklin's map of the Gulf Stream is the earliest known map of its kind. It enabled ship captains to cut as much as two weeks off their Atlantic sailing time.

While Franklin and Temple were on the high seas, America's Revolutionary War began in Massachusetts. Landing in Philadelphia, Franklin learned that fighting had broken out between American militiamen and British redcoats at Lexington and Concord on April 19, 1775. During a daylong battle, the Americans had chased the redcoats back to their base in Boston and blockaded all roads leading out of town.

A newspaper editor met Franklin at the dock. "Dr. Franklin…says we have no favors to expect from the [British] ministry," the editor reported. "Nothing but submission will satisfy them.... [He] is highly pleased to find us arming and preparing for the worst events."

The day after he arrived, Franklin was elected as one of Pennsylvania's delegates to the Second Continental Congress, about to meet in Philadelphia. At sixty-nine, he was by far the oldest member of the congress.

Franklin was assigned to several committees. He attended every session of both the Continental Congress and the Pennsylvania Assembly, which was meeting at the same time. "My time was never more fully employed," he told a friend. "In the morning at 6, I am at the committee of safety, appointed by the assembly to put the province in a state of defense, which [meets] till near 9, when I am at the congress, and that sits till after 4 in the afternoon."

Despite the outbreak of fighting and the continuing blockade of Boston, most of the congressional delegates still hoped for a peaceful settlement. They were not yet willing to declare independence.

Franklin believed that it was too late for any reconciliation with England. He kept his views to himself at first, listening to the debates, saying little, at times dozing in his chair. But when the Battle of Bunker Hill was fought in Boston, and British warships bombarded Charleston, South Carolina, both in June 1775, he was one of the first delegates to speak out in favor of immediate independence. "Words and arguments are now of no use," he said.

Throughout the colonies, Americans were beginning to take sides. Those who supported the king and wanted to remain British subjects were known as Loyalists. Colonists who favored independence called themselves Patriots. Deeply felt political differences led to bitter arguments and lasting resentments between friends and even among members of the same family.

Franklin had labored for years to preserve the empire. Rebuffed by British officials and personally humiliated in the Cockpit—"treated as the cause of the mischief I was laboring to prevent"— he now believed that only through independence could Americans retain their liberties. He became one of the most ardent Patriots in the Continental Congress. "He does not hesitate at our boldest measure," delegate John Adams of Massachusetts told his wife, Abigail, "but rather seems to think us, too irresolute, and backward."

When Franklin tried to win over his son to the revolutionary cause, the close relationship they had always enjoyed was shattered. William refused to side with his father. As governor of New

Franklin's son, New Jersey colonial governor William Franklin, was arrested and imprisoned when he sided with the British against the American rebels.

Jersey, appointed by the king, he remained a keen supporter of royal authority. Meetings between father and son in the summer of 1775 ended in shouting matches loud enough to alarm the neighbors. From then on, they were barely on speaking terms.

William tried to persuade the New Jersey Assembly to arrange a separate peace with Britain. The assembly, in turn, ordered his arrest as "an enemy of the liberties of this country," and the congress voted to have him imprisoned in Connecticut. Franklin made no attempt to intervene on his son's behalf. Eventually William was exchanged for an American prisoner. He spent the war years as an unapologetic Loyalist in British-occupied New York, while his father, a dedicated Patriot, devoted his energies to the fight for independence.

The Continental Congress sent Franklin on two important missions. In October 1775, he was named head of a delegation that traveled to Cambridge, Massachusetts, for a weeklong conference with George Washington, who had been named commander in chief of the Continental Army. British troops were still holed up in Boston—under deadly fire, if they showed themselves, from American sharpshooters. During the trip, Franklin had dinner one night with fellow congressman John Adams and his wife, Abigail. "From my infancy," she wrote, "I had been taught to venerate [him]. I found him social but not talkative, and when he spoke something useful dropped from his tongue. He was grave, yet pleasant and affable."

In March 1776, at the age of seventy, Franklin headed another delegation that made an arduous journey over frozen roads to Canada, where they hoped to persuade the Canadians to join the American rebellion. At Saratoga, New York, the congressmen had to wait a week for ice on the lakes to clear. Moving by flatboat and on horseback deeper into the America wilderness than Franklin had ever been before, they slept in the woods and on the floors of abandoned houses. Franklin worried that he might not survive the hardships of the trip. "I have undertaken a fatigue that at my time of life may prove too much for me," he wrote to a friend. By the time the delegation reached Montreal, he "suffered much from a number of large boils [and] my legs swelled."

Montreal, Canada, as it appeared in the 1770s when Franklin traveled there in a failed attempt to win French Canadians to the American cause.

A Perspective View of MONTREAL in Canada.

An American force sent north to invade Canada had captured Montreal but had bogged down outside Quebec City. The Americans had not been equipped for a Canadian winter. They were hungry, sick, and cold, and "must starve, plunder, or surrender," Franklin reported. His delegation failed to gain support from the local Canadians. Learning that British reinforcements were on the way, they announced "our firm and unanimous opinion that it is better immediately to withdraw."

Back in Philadelphia after the hopeless two-month Canadian expedition, Franklin was worn out. Confined to bed with painful boils and gout, he felt so exhausted he did not leave the house for days. But he perked up when the congress invited him to join yet another committee. This time he was to help draft the statement we know today as the Declaration of Independence.

Thirty-three-year-old Thomas Jefferson, the youngest member of the five-man committee, was chosen to write the first draft of the declaration. He worked on the draft for two weeks, writing and rewriting. When he had a passage that he particularly liked, or one that he questioned, he would send it over to Franklin's house for comments. "Will Doctor Franklin be so good as to peruse it and suggest such alterations as his more enlarged view of the subject will dictate?" he asked in one covering note.

After a lifetime as a writer and editor, Franklin knew good writing when he saw it, and he treated Jefferson's draft gently, suggesting a number of small changes. Where Jefferson had written "We hold these truths to be sacred and undeniable," Franklin suggested "We hold these truths to be self-evident."

On July 2, 1776, the congress voted in favor of independence. The delegates then spent the next two days going over the declaration word by word, making almost a hundred additional changes before they were satisfied. The final version of the Declaration of Independence was approved unanimously on July 4.

The outcome of the Revolutionary War would determine whether the signers of that declaration—the fifty-six members of the Second Continental Congress—would be honored by future generations as the founders of a new nation, or be hanged by the British for treason.

According to a story that was first recorded many years later, John Hancock, president of the congress, urged a unanimous vote by telling the delegates: "There must be no pulling different ways. We must all hang together." To which Franklin reportedly replied, "Yes, we must indeed all hang together, or most assuredly, we shall all hang separately."

Benjamin Franklin, John Adams, and Thomas Jefferson discuss a draft of the Declaration of Independence at Jefferson's lodgings in Philadelphia. An early twentieth-century painting by Jean Leon Gerome Ferris.

BECOMING BEN FRANKLIN

Benjamin Franklin signs the Declaration of Independence. From a 1911 painting by Charles E. Mills.

✳ ✳ ✳

On August 27, six weeks after the declaration was announced to the world, Washington's army was defeated at the Battle of Long Island and sent retreating across the Hudson River to New Jersey and beyond. Admiral Richard Howe, commander of the British forces in America, sent a note to the Continental Congress suggesting that reconciliation with England might still be possible. He asked the congress to send a delegation to meet with him in a private conference at his headquarters on Staten Island. The congress selected three of its members—Franklin, John Adams, and Edward Rutledge of South Carolina—to attend the meeting under a flag of truce and listen to what Admiral Howe had to say.

On their way to the meeting, the three delegates found the roads crowded with soldiers and other travelers, and the inns full. Stopping for the night at New Brunswick, New Jersey, Franklin and Adams had to share a room with one bed and a single small window. The window was open. Adams, recovering from an illness, was afraid of the night air. He immediately slammed the window shut.

"Oh!" exclaimed Franklin. "Don't shut the window. We shall be suffocated."

"I answered I was afraid of the evening air," Adams recalled.

"Dr. Franklin replied, 'The air within this chamber will soon be, and indeed is now, worse than that without doors. Come! Open the window and come to bed, and I will convince you. I believe you are not acquainted with my theory of colds.'

"Opening the window and leaping into bed, I said I had read his letters to Dr. Cooper in which he had advanced that nobody ever got a cold by going into a cold church, or any other cold air."

At a time when viruses were unknown, Franklin, who was still taking his air baths at the age of seventy, had guessed correctly that colds are passed from person to person. Adams didn't believe it, because "the theory was so little consistent with my experience… [but] I had so much curiosity to hear his reasons that I would run the risk of a cold.

"The Doctor then began a harangue, upon air and cold and respiration and perspiration, with which I was so much amused that I soon fell asleep," while Franklin, who enjoyed nothing more than expounding on his scientific theories, continued happily to talk.

The meeting with Howe the following day was, as it turned out, a waste of time. The British commander suggested a return to the peaceful accommodation that had existed between Britain and her American colonies before 1765. But it was too late for that. America had already declared independence. "The three gentlemen," Howe reported, "were very explicit in their opinion that the associated colonies would not [agree] to any peace or alliance but as free and independent states."

While independence had indeed been *declared*, it had not yet been *won*. Great Britain had the most powerful army and navy on earth. George Washington was in command of a ragged army of volunteers with little training and not enough gunpowder to keep their muskets firing. Franklin, along with many Americans, believed that the rebels would need help from abroad to defeat the British. The congress had already appointed Franklin to a Committee of Secret Correspondence, which was assigned to seek foreign support for the united colonies.

Admiral Howe and the British did not yet know that the Americans had secretly asked the French government for aid.

John Adams, Edward Rutledge, and Benjamin Franklin meet with British admiral Richard Howe.

Chapter Eight

An American in Paris

D. BENJAMIN FRANKLIN
et vita inter Americanos acta,
et magnis electricitatis periculis clarus.

Franklin was approaching his seventy-first birthday when he set out on the most important mission of his life. The Continental Congress had appointed him to join Silas Deane and Arthur Lee as a three-man commission in Paris to seek urgently needed aid from the government of France.

France and England had been fighting on and off for centuries. France had not forgotten its humiliating loss of Canada to England in the French and Indian War. The French government watched for any opportunity to undermine the British Empire and regain its foothold in North America.

At the moment, however, France and England were at peace. The young French king, Louis XVI, wasn't prepared to side openly with the rebellious Americans. The outcome of their war for independence remained very much in doubt. George Washington's bedraggled army had not yet won a significant victory. It was clear that without foreign aid, the Americans could not hope to overcome British power. Franklin and his fellow commissioners faced the daunting challenge of persuading France to join the war as America's ally.

Franklin in Paris, wearing his bifocals and fur hat. A 1780 engraving by Johann Elias Haid, after a painting by Cochin.

Franklin sailed to Europe with his two grandsons, Temple, now sixteen, and seven-year-old Benny Bache, the son of Franklin's daughter. They arrived in Paris just before Christmas in 1776, after a rough and risky ocean crossing. If prowling British cruisers had captured their ship, Franklin would have been arrested at sea, imprisoned in England, and possibly hanged for high treason. As it was, he suffered from boils, rashes, and swollen joints during the stormy voyage; his weeks at sea "almost demolished me."

In Paris Franklin was greeted as a hero—the American scientist famous for his electrical discoveries who had come to France in the name of liberty. "Doctor Franklin is mightily run after [and] much feted," reported one observer. "He has a most pleasing expression, very little hair, and a fur cap which he keeps constantly on his head."

France had been swept up in an outpouring of popular enthusiasm for the American Revolution. Paris cafés buzzed with excitement for the American cause, French aristocrats sang songs in praise of liberty, and idealistic young noblemen volunteered to sail to America and join the rebels. "All men have equal rights to liberty!" cried the celebrated French philosopher Voltaire.

Franklin was introduced to Voltaire at a meeting of the French Academy of Science. At first, the two elderly sages bowed politely to each other. That wasn't good enough for the academy's members, so Franklin and Voltaire clasped hands. But the crowd demanded that they embrace in true French fashion. So they "then embraced each other by hugging one another in their arms and kissing each other's cheeks, and then the tumult subsided," reported John Adams, who had replaced Silas Deane as one of the American commissioners in Paris.

Franklin was invited to live at a wealthy merchant's spacious estate in

Voltaire: French philosopher and passionate apostle of liberty.

The village of Passy outside Paris. Franklin lived here for nearly nine years as an American representative to the court of France. Painting by Nicolas Jean Baptiste Raguenot.

Passy, a leafy village just outside Paris. This was to be Franklin's home for nearly nine years as he worked to win French support and negotiate a peace treaty with England. He had his own comfortable house, a staff of uniformed servants, and outside his door a formal terraced garden with walking paths overlooking the River Seine and the rooftops of Paris beyond. Temple served as his grandfather's personal secretary. Franklin had a lightning rod erected on the roof of his house, a printing press installed in the basement, and a wine cellar stocked with a thousand bottles, which he maintained for the steady stream of guests who came to call.

As the world's most famous American and a champion of liberty, he was "much sought after and entertained," reported an observer, "not only by his learned colleagues, but by everyone who can gain access to him." Wherever he went, crowds gathered, hoping to catch a glimpse of him. Portraits of Franklin appeared everywhere, on snuffboxes and candy boxes, on dishes, handkerchiefs, and pocket-knives. "My face," he wrote to his sister, "is now almost as well known as that of the moon."

In the eyes of the French, Franklin seemed to represent everything that fascinated them about the New World of America. They were charmed by his lively, ungrammatical French. He dressed simply, appearing in public as a modest, homespun sage. Instead of the short sword worn by aristocrats, he carried his cane. And in place of a fashionable powdered wig, he favored the soft fur cap

FRANKLIN'S RECEPTION AT THE COURT OF FRANCE, 1778.
RESPECTFULLY DEDICATED TO THE PEOPLE OF THE UNITED STATES.

Franklin's reception at the French court, as imagined by the nineteenth-century artist Anton Hohenstein. Franklin appeared at court wearing his plain brown suit. A laurel wreath is being placed upon his wigless head. French notables surround him, while Marie-Antoinette and Louis XVI remain seated.

59

he had picked up on his trip to Canada, which he pulled down low, almost to his spectacles. When he was received at the court of Louis XVI, he appeared in a plain brown velvet suit. "I should have taken him for a big farmer," observed one onlooker, "so great was his contrast with the elaborate outfits of the other diplomats who were all powdered, in full dress, and splashed all over with gold and ribbons."

Life in France agreed with Franklin. "I never remember [seeing] my grandfather in better health," wrote Temple. "The air of Passy and the warm bath three times a week [at a luxurious bathhouse on the Seine] have made quite a young man of him. His pleasing gaiety makes everybody in love with him, especially the ladies, who permit him always to kiss them."

Franklin still had an eye for the ladies, and during his years in France he enjoyed affectionate friendships with glamorous female admirers who flirted with him, composed music for him, played chess with him, and addressed him as *mon cher Papa*—my dear Papa. "You have taken in my heart the place of [my] father," confided Madame Brillon de Jouy, an accomplished harpsichordist and "one of the most beautiful women in Paris," according to John Adams. Franklin was so taken with Madame Anne-Catherine Helvetius, a vivacious widow who entertained artists and intellectuals in her salon, that he proposed marriage. She declined but remained a devoted friend.

How seriously Franklin intended his proposal is uncertain. But there is no question that his playful flirtations helped him feel like a younger man. "I do not find that I grow any older," he told a friend. "Being arrived at seventy, and considering that by traveling further in the same road I should probably be led to the grave, I stopped short, turned about, and walked back again, which having done these four years, you may now call me sixty-six."

Franklin wrote humorous essays and fables for the amusement of his French friends, and printed them on his basement press. And he found time to perfect one of his most useful inventions, bifocal glasses, "double spectacles" as he called them. Tired of needing two pairs of glasses—one for reading, the other for seeing at a distance—he had his lenses cut and half of each lens placed in the same frame. "By this means," he wrote, "I wear my spectacles constantly. I have only to move my eyes up or down, as I want to see distinctly far or near, the proper lenses always being ready."

Franklin's grandson Benny attended a boarding school in Switzerland and visited Paris during summer holidays. Franklin gave the boy swimming lessons in the Seine and, when he was thirteen, arranged to have him trained as a printer. Benny told a visitor that Franklin was "very different from other old persons, for they are fretful and complaining and dissatisfied, and my grandpa is laughing and cheerful like a young person."

Franklin's American colleagues complained about his chaotic record-keeping and his busy social life. He spent too much time dining out and enjoying himself, they said. "He was invited to dine every day and never declined unless we had invited company to dine with us," grumbled John Adams. "And he came home at all hours from nine to twelve o'clock at night."

Franklin's French friends were more approving: "He would eat, sleep, work whenever he saw fit, according to his needs," one of them said, "so that there was never a more leisurely man, though he certainly handled a tremendous amount of business."

The business at hand was proving far more difficult than the Americans had expected. By the fall of 1777, British troops had captured Philadelphia, now America's largest city and the proud capital of the embattled colonies. Washington's beleaguered army was short of everything it needed to survive the coming winter. France had been secretly supplying the rebels with arms and money, but Louis XVI and his ministers were not convinced that they should enter into an open alliance with an untried little nation an ocean away.

Franklin and his fellow commissioners had their work cut out for them. Their mission was to bring France into the war on America's side. Yet the commissioners often disagreed among themselves. Their disputes clouded their common purpose. And they did not suspect that their trusted secretary, Edward Bancroft, was actually a British spy—as historians discovered a century later when they uncovered secret documents in London archives.

Bancroft, a longtime friend of both Franklin and Silas Deane, had been recruited by the British secret service as one of its many spies in Paris. He sent in his reports by writing in invisible ink between the lines of fake love letters, stuffing the letters into a bottle and dropping the bottle into a hollow at the foot of a tree in the Tuileries Gardens, where it was picked up after dark by a messenger from the British embassy.

As outlandish as this scheme may seem today, it worked. Bancroft's secret reports, hundreds of them, kept the British government fully informed on discussions the Americans were having with French officials. Franklin and Deane trusted Bancroft so completely that they sent him to London

Fellow commissioner John Adams complained that Franklin was disorganized and much too fond of dinner parties.

BECOMING
BEN FRANKLIN

The French foreign minister, the Comte de
Vergennes. He established a bond of friendship
and trust with Franklin.

to gather intelligence there. When he returned to Paris, he brought false information planted by his British spymasters.

Although Franklin didn't suspect Bancroft, he knew that Paris was a hotbed of spies. "You are surrounded by spies who watch your every movement," an American friend living in Paris warned him. Franklin skillfully used this knowledge by playing on French fears that the Americans and the British might patch up their differences and get back together.

The French foreign minister, the Comte de Vergennes, had turned down American proposals for an immediate alliance. He was waiting to see how the Revolutionary War would play out. As Vergennes hesitated, an American messenger, Jonathan Austin, rode into Franklin's courtyard with word that the rebels had won their first major battlefield victory, at Saratoga, New York. British General John Burgoyne had surrendered with thousands of his troops, marking a crucial turning point in the course of the war. The British were not invincible, after all. Franklin was jubilant, clapping his hands and exclaiming, "Oh! Mr. Austin, you have brought us glorious news!"

According to one account, Franklin wept with joy. But he kept a cool head. He recognized the surprise American victory as an opportunity to prod the French.

Franklin agreed to meet with a British envoy who had come to Paris to sound out the Americans on a new peace proposal. The British were prepared to offer everything the rebels wanted, short of independence. Franklin wasn't sure who was spying on whom, but he knew that the French, through their own spy network, would learn that the Americans were holding peace discussions with the British envoy. And he would let the British know how close the Americans were to an agreement with the French. "They play us off against one another," warned the British ambassador to France. "Franklin's natural subtlety gives him a great advantage in such a game."

Franklin's shrewd double-edged diplomacy worked like a charm. The French quickly agreed to recognize the independence of the United States. They offered to sign two treaties with the new nation, one creating a military alliance, the other an agreement on friendship and trade. Without Franklin's maneuvers, confessed the French minister of state, there would have been no treaties.

At the signing ceremony on February 6, 1778, Franklin wore a faded and worn blue velvet coat, "to give it a little revenge," he explained. It was the same coat he had worn as he stood in the Cockpit four years earlier and silently endured a dressing-down by the British prosecutor.

With the signing of the treaties, Franklin's fellow commissioners went home. At France's insistence, he remained as the sole American representative in Paris. He had established a bond of trust and goodwill with the French foreign minister. Vergennes preferred to deal only with Franklin, who continued to negotiate for more aid.

Franklin's efforts were backed by the Marquis de Lafayette, a young French nobleman who had volunteered to fight with Washington's army. Lafayette had been wounded at the Battle of Brandywine and had spent the winter with Washington at Valley Forge. He had now returned home and was using his considerable influence at court to rally French military support for the Revolution.

Washington's revived army had at last gone on the offensive. During the summer of 1780, French reinforcements sailed to America to bolster the American cause. The war's decisive battle was fought at Yorktown, Virginia, where French warships and troops joined with the American

A meeting between Franklin and the Marquis de Lafayette, as imagined by the nineteenth-century Italian artist, Anibale Gatti.

army under General Washington. The British commander, Lord Charles Cornwallis, and his redcoats found themselves besieged on the Yorktown peninsula. They held out for three weeks before surrendering to the Americans and their French allies on October 19, 1781. When the British prime minister, Lord North, learned that Cornwallis had surrendered, he exclaimed, "Oh God. It is all over. It is all over."

British general Charles Cornwallis surrenders to the allied French and American forces at Yorktown, 1781. An 1870 engraving.

Franklin's success in persuading the French to advance the Americans loan after loan, and his persistence in urging France to support the rebels with warships and ground troops, were crucial to the ultimate American victory in the War of Independence.

His work in Paris was not yet finished. Along with John Adams and John Jay, Franklin served as a member of the delegation that negotiated a peace treaty with Britain. "I hope we shall agree and not be long about it," he said. However, the negotiations lasted more than a year. On September 3, 1783, Great Britain and the United States signed the Treaty of Paris, officially ending the Revolutionary War and declaring the United States "to be free, sovereign and independent."

Once again, by helping to negotiate peace with England while retaining the friendship of France, Franklin proved himself a masterful diplomat. "There never was a good war," he told a friend, "or a bad peace."

That year Franklin had an opportunity to witness the first manned balloon flights. French experimenters had begun filling enormous silk balloons with heated air or hydrogen gas and sending them aloft. Wicker baskets carrying human passengers dangled from some of the balloons, which ascended three thousand feet and traveled for miles as astonished spectators craned their necks to gaze skyward and marvel at humanity's conquest of the air. Franklin had great expectations

Conquest of the air: From his terrace in Passy, Franklin witnessed history's first manned balloon flights in 1783.

for the future of manned flight. When a skeptic asked, "What good were these experiments?" Franklin replied, "What good is a new-born babe?"

By now, he was anxious to return to America. "The French are an amiable people to live with," he said. "They love me, and I love them, yet I do not feel myself at home."

Even so, the Continental Congress kept Franklin in Paris as official ambassador of the newly independent republic. He managed to coax yet another loan from the nearly bankrupt French government; he negotiated a treaty of friendship and commerce with Sweden, America's first with a foreign power; he had the constitutions of the newly United States translated into French, the only language in which they could be widely read.

After nearly nine years in France, the congress accepted Franklin's resignation. He was seventy-nine now and increasingly plagued by painful attacks of gout and kidney stones. "I have continued to work until late in the day," he wrote to his sister Jane, "'tis time I should go home, and go to bed."

Thomas Jefferson was named to take Franklin's place as American ambassador to France. When asked "Is it you, Sir, who replaces Dr. Franklin?" he always replied, "No one can *replace* him, Sir; I am only his successor."

"Oh that great man, that poor dear man," cried Madame Helvetius, to whom Franklin had proposed, "we will never see him again!"

Before sailing for home, Franklin attended to a family matter. His son, William, who had remained loyal to England, was now living in London. William wrote to his father seeking reconciliation. Franklin's guarded reply expressed his lingering pain at their estrangement and his deeply personal commitment to the Revolution: "Nothing has ever hurt me so much...as to find myself deserted in my old age by my only son; and not only deserted, but to find him taking up arms against me, in a cause wherein my good fame, fortune and life were all at stake."

Father and son met for several days at Southampton, England, the port from which Franklin would sail on his eighth and final Atlantic crossing. Their meeting was civil but cool as they settled family business matters. Then they parted for good.

Before their final meeting, William had pleaded that as governor of New Jersey, he had "acted from a strong sense of...duty to my king." He could not apologize, since he would act no differ-

William Franklin met briefly with his father in Southampton, England, to settle family business affairs. Father and son never communicated again. Portrait by Mather Brown.

ently if it were all to happen again. "If I have been mistaken," he wrote, "I cannot help it." Franklin wasn't convinced. *"There are Natural Duties,"* he argued, *"which precede political ones, and cannot be extinguished by them"* (Franklin's emphasis).

William was not invited to the farewell party aboard Franklin's ship. The next morning, Franklin set sail, taking his grandsons Benny and Temple, William's son, back to America with him.

Franklin never communicated with his son again.

Chapter Nine

A Useful Life

Accompanied by his grandsons Temple and Benny, Franklin arrived at Philadelphia's Market Street wharf on September 14, 1785. Sixty-two years earlier he had stepped ashore at the same spot and wandered alone up Market Street, a friendless seventeen-year-old runaway. This time he was

Franklin returns to Philadelphia in 1785, greeted by his daughter, Sally, her family, and friends. Painting by Jean Leon Gerome Ferris.

greeted by booming cannons, pealing bells, and a cheering crowd that lined the wharf and escorted him, his face bathed in tears, to the courtyard of his Market Street home.

At the age of seventy-nine, Franklin might have been expected to retire from public life and enjoy a well-earned rest. But he was no sooner back in America than he was elected president of the Pennsylvania Executive Council, making him, in effect, governor of the state.

He could not resist this latest honor. "Old as I am," he confessed, "I am not yet grown insensible with respect to reputation." He was unanimously reelected twice, in 1786 and 1787, a vote of confidence, he told his sister, that "flatters my vanity much more than a peerage could do."

At home, surrounded by members of his family, Franklin was "as happy as I could wish." Living with him were his daughter, Sally, her husband, Richard Bache, and their children, four "little prattlers who cling about the knees of their grandpapa and afford me great pleasure." He took great pleasure, too, in building a printing house for Benny, who had learned printing in France and now followed in his grandfather's footsteps to become a full-time Philadelphia printer and publisher.

To accommodate his growing family, Franklin enlarged his house. He added a new wing that included a dining room big enough to seat twenty-four, and a library with floor-to-ceiling shelves that held his collection of four thousand books, along with his electrical equipment, a glass machine that displayed the flow of blood through the human body, and a rolling press he had invented for copying letters. For reading, he built a big, comfortable rocking chair with an overhead fan that was operated with a foot pedal. He was especially proud of the mechanical arm he designed, a long pole with a pair of pincers at the end, which could pluck books from upper shelves and then replace them.

To help keep his ailments at bay, Franklin watched his diet, worked out daily with dumbbells, and enjoyed his daily air baths. Members of the American Philosophical Society, which he had founded some forty years earlier, came to hold meetings in his new dining room. He enjoyed playing cards with friends. He fretted about wasting time, but at his age, he figured, he could relax a little, so "satisfied with a small reason when it is in favor of doing what I have a mind to, I shuffle the cards again, and begin another game."

On fine days, visitors gathered in Franklin's garden. "We found him in his garden, sitting... under a very large mulberry tree, with several other gentlemen and two or three ladies," one visitor reported. "The tea table was spread under the tree, and Mrs. Bache, who is the only daughter of the Doctor, and lives with him, served it out to the company. She had three of her children about her. They seemed excessively fond of their grandpa."

During these years, Franklin resumed work on the autobiography he had started years earlier. With age came the knowledge that he could not always live up to the standards of conduct he laid down for himself as a young man, and set forth at length in his autobiography, no matter how dili-

Relaxing under the mulberry tree in Franklin's Philadelphia garden.

gently he tried. On virtues such as *Industry*, *Frugality*, and *Resolution*, he could give himself high marks. But when it came to such qualities as *Humility* ("I cannot boast of much success in acquiring…this virtue"), or *Vanity* and *Pride*, he had to admit that he had fallen far short of moral perfection.

"There is perhaps no one of our natural passions so hard to subdue as *Pride,*" he wrote. "Disguise it, struggle with it, beat it down, stifle it, mortify it as much as one pleases, it is still alive, and will every now and then peep out and show itself. . . . Even if I could conceive that I had completely overcome it, I should probably [be] proud of my humility."

Experience had taught him "that a perfect character might be attended with the inconvenience of being envied and hated." A wise person "should allow a few faults in himself," or risk losing his friends. And while Franklin had not always succeeded, he didn't regret his efforts to strive for moral perfection. "Though I never arrived at the perfection I had been so ambitious of obtaining, but fell far short of it, yet I was by the endeavor a better and happier man than I otherwise should have been, if I had not attempted it."

✳ ✳ ✳

Franklin's yearning for perfection was frustrated once again when he attended the Constitutional Convention held in Philadelphia during the summer of 1787. The Articles of Confederation, signed by the individual states in the early days of the Revolution, had proved too weak to hold the new nation together. The Continental Congress had called for the Philadelphia convention to draft a new and stronger constitution that would unite the states and meet the nation's pressing needs.

Fifty-five delegates from every state except Rhode Island (which refused to attend) gathered in Philadelphia for sixteen weeks of speeches, debates, negotiations, and compromise as they discussed how best to govern themselves. At eighty-one, Franklin was the oldest delegate by far, twice as old as the average age of those in attendance. A fellow delegate described him as "a short, fat, trunched old man in a plain Quaker dress, bald pate, and short white locks."

The delegates met in the Pennsylvania State House (now called Independence Hall), where Franklin had served for so many years as an assemblyman. Since his gout and kidney stones made it painful for him to walk, he was carried to the daily sessions in a sedan chair he had brought from Paris—a chair balanced on long poles held aloft by four husky prisoners from the Walnut Street jail.

*Franklin holds forth at the
Constitutional Convention.*

Helped from his sedan chair, he took his seat every morning at one of the fourteen round tables in the East Room of the State House. And he attended faithfully, several hours a day for four months.

He listened attentively, but didn't speak often. When he had something to say, he wrote out his speech and asked a fellow delegate to read it aloud, since he found it difficult to stand for any length of time. As always, he was in his element among small, informal groups, but he had never liked to make speeches. "He is no speaker," one delegate observed. "He is, however, a most extraordinary man, and tells a story in a style more engaging than anything I ever heard.... He is eighty-two [actually eighty-one] and possesses an activity of mind equal to a youth of twenty-five."

The delegates had plenty of tough issues to resolve. Their debates were heated and prolonged as they tried to balance the conflicting demands of large states and small ones, rich states and poor ones, slave states and free states. The torrid weather in Philadelphia that summer didn't help matters. Along with the stifling heat and humidity, giant flies and mosquitoes invaded the State House; they could bite right through the delegates' long silk stockings.

Franklin worked to encourage a spirit of compromise. "We are sent here to consult, not to contend with each other," he said. Many of his own legislative proposals were rejected. The delegates listened to him respectfully, but they did not necessarily follow his advice. His main contribution was bringing opposing delegates together, allowing tempers to cool, and getting them to agree. "We are making experiments in politics," he told a friend. "We must not expect that a new government may be formed ... without a fault."

The thorniest issue at the Constitutional Convention concerned the future of slavery in America. Many of the delegates were opposed to slavery. But delegates from the South, where plantations and their owners' wealth depended on slave labor, threatened to walk out of the convention if the proposed constitution outlawed slavery. Bowing to what they viewed as political reality, the delegates finally agreed to an uneasy compromise. The slave trade would be banned as of the year 1808. But the institution of slavery itself would be tolerated under the new constitution, each state deciding the issue for itself.

Throughout Franklin's life, most whites in America had accepted slavery as a matter of course. Even in Philadelphia, a northern city, almost ten percent of the population in 1760 was made up

of black slaves. At one time, Franklin himself had owned slaves who worked as his household servants. But attitudes were changing, and by the time of the Constitutional Convention, Franklin had come to detest slavery, calling it "a practice that has so long disgraced our nation and religion."

The constitution that the delegates finally agreed to sign was the result of many compromises, including on the issue of slavery. And just as Franklin did not expect perfection in himself, he didn't expect it in the art of government. When he rose to his painful feet to deliver some closing remarks, he paid tribute to the spirit of cooperation that had made the new constitution possible.

"I confess that there are several parts of this new constitution which I do not at present approve," Franklin said. "But I am not sure that I shall never approve them, for having lived long, I have experienced many instances of being obliged by better information or fuller consideration to change [my] opinions even on important subjects.... The older I grow, the more apt I am to doubt my own judgment, and to pay attention to the judgment of others."

Franklin doubted whether any convention could have agreed on a better document. "Thus I consent, sir," he concluded, "to this constitution, because I expect no better, and because I am not sure that it is not the best." He urged his fellow delegates to join him in signing the document, "for our own sakes as part of the people, and for the sake of posterity."

Franklin became the only Founding Father to sign all four of the documents that led to the creation of the United States: the Declaration of Independence, the treaty of alliance with France, the peace treaty with England, and the Constitution of the United States.

The Constitution, which vests all power in "We the People," has proved to be the most successful document of its kind ever written. It is the oldest written constitution still in use by any nation in the world, and we today are "the People" for whom it was intended.

As Franklin approached the end of his life, he turned to the one great issue that could not be solved by any compromise. In 1787, while the Constitutional Convention was still in session, he accepted the presidency of the first group in North America to work for the eradication of slavery—the Pennsylvania Society for Promoting the Abolition of Slavery. Though his health was failing, he devoted himself to the society's mission of emancipating slaves and helping them enter a free society.

In 1790, Franklin sent a formal petition to the new federal Congress, attacking slavery and ask-

Signing the Constitution. George Washington presides while Franklin and Thomas Jefferson are seated. A twentieth-century painting by Howard Chandler Christy, currently on display in the United States Capitol.

ing that "the blessings of liberty" guaranteed by the Constitution be granted "without distinction of color ... to those unhappy men who alone in this land of freedom are degraded into perpetual bondage." The petition was rejected on the grounds that Congress had no authority to interfere in the internal affairs of the individual states. And it was denounced by Representative James Jackson of Georgia, who declared that slavery was sanctioned by the Bible, and that troublemakers like

Benjamin Franklin were a threat to the social order. Slavery in the United States would continue until America's Civil War and Abraham Lincoln's Emancipation Proclamation of 1863.

Franklin's anti-slavery petition was his last public act. Two months later, he lay on his deathbed as friends and family members moved in and out of the room, saying their good-byes. Franklin reached out to take the hand of his grandson, his namesake Benny, whom he had taught to swim and had trained as a printer. We are told that he held Benny's hand for a very long time.

That evening, April 17, 1790, Benjamin Franklin passed away at the age of eighty-four. He had told his mother once that when his life was over, "I would rather have it said, 'He lived usefully' than 'He died rich.'"

Two centuries after Franklin's time, we remember him as a printer, editor, and publisher; a community organizer; a scientist and inventor; a statesman, humorist, and philosopher; and an influential writer. His contributions to society include a library, a university, a fire company, a philosophical society, the lightning rod, the Franklin stove, and bifocal glasses. And he helped give birth to a new kind of nation, ruled not by a hereditary monarch but by "We, the People."

"He snatched lightning from the sky," said the French statesman Jacques Turgot, "and the scepter from tyrants."

Franklin at rest, his hat, book, and papers on the table, and in the background, through an open door, ships at dock. Engraving after a 1780 painting by Louis Carrogis Carmentelle.

Time Line

1706	Benjamin Franklin is born in Boston on January 17.
1716	Begins working in his father's soap- and candle-making shop.
1718	Apprenticed to his brother James, a printer.
1723	Runs away to Philadelphia. Finds work with Samuel Keimer.
1724	Sails to London, England, where he finds work in printing shops.
1726	Returns to Philadelphia and Keimer's printing shop.
1727	First meeting of the discussion group the Junto.
1728	Opens his own printing shop with a partner.
1729	Buys *The Pennsylvania Gazette*. Son William is born around this time, mother unknown.
1730	Dissolves partnership and starts his own printing business. Marries Deborah Read.
1731	Founds Library Company of Philadelphia, America's first lending library.
1732	Another son, Francis Folger, is born.
1733	Publishes first edition of *Poor Richard's Almanack*.
1736	Appointed clerk of the Pennsylvania Assembly. Francis dies of smallpox at age four. Union Fire Company is formed.
1737	Appointed Philadelphia postmaster.
1739–40	Invents and perfects "Pennsylvania fireplace" ("Franklin stove").
1743	Founds American Philosophical Society. Daughter Sarah ("Sally") is born.
1746–47	Begins electricity experiments.
1748	Retires from active printing business.
1749	Proposes Academy of Philadelphia (now University of Pennsylvania).
1751	Publishes electricity experiments. Pennsylvania Hospital chartered. Elected to Pennsylvania Assembly.
1752	Performs famous kite experiment and invents lightning rod.
1753	Appointed deputy postmaster general of North America. Receives honorary degrees from Harvard and Yale.
1754	French and Indian War begins. Attends Albany Conference and proposes a plan to unite the colonies.

1757–62	Sails to London, where he lives as representative of the Pennsylvania Assembly. Receives honorary degrees from University of St. Andrews and Oxford University.
1762	Returns to Philadelphia. William is appointed royal governor of New Jersey.
1764	Denounces massacre of Indians. Elected speaker of the Pennsylvania Assembly, then loses seat in a bitter election campaign. Returns to London as agent for Pennsylvania and later as agent for Georgia, New Jersey, and Massachusetts.
1765	Parliament passes the Stamp Act.
1766	Testifies against the Stamp Act before the House of Commons.
1767	Townshend duties imposed, including a tax on tea.
1771	Begins *Autobiography*.
1773	Parliament passes the Tea Act, retaining the hated tax on tea. On December 16, the Boston Tea Party dumps 342 chests of tea into the harbor.
1774	Summoned before the privy council in the Cockpit and denounced. Dismissed as deputy postmaster general. "Intolerable Acts" ignite a colonial crisis. Deborah dies in Philadelphia at age sixty-six.
1775	Returns to Philadelphia. Learns of Battles of Lexington and Concord on April 19. Elected to the Second Continental Congress. Visits Washington's camp at Cambridge.
1776	Futile mission to Canada. Helps write Declaration of Independence. Meets with Lord Howe on Staten Island. Sails to France with grandsons, Temple and Benny.
1776–85	Lives in Passy, outside Paris, as an American commissioner to the French court.
1778	Treaties of alliance and of friendship and commerce between France and the United States are signed.
1779	Becomes the sole American commissioner to the French court.
1781	British army under Cornwallis surrenders at Yorktown.
1782–83	With John Adams and John Jay, Franklin negotiates a peace treaty with Britain.
1785	Last meeting with William. Sails back to Philadelphia. Elected president of the Pennsylvania Executive Council.
1787	Attends the Constitutional Convention. Elected president of the Pennsylvania Society for Promoting the Abolition of Slavery.
1790	Dies on April 17 at the age of eighty-four.

Source Notes

The following notes refer to the sources of quoted material. Each citation includes the first and last words or phrases of the quotation and the source. Unless otherwise noted, all references are to works cited in the Selected Bibliography. Certain primary documents are referenced separately following the applicable quotation.

Abbreviations used:

Almanack—*Wit and Wisdom from Poor Richard's Almanack*

Autobiography—Benjamin Franklin, *Autobiography*

Bowen—Catherine Drinker Bowen, *The Most Dangerous Man in America*

Brands—H.W. Brands, *The First American*

Isaacson—Walter Isaacson, *Benjamin Franklin, An American Life*

Liberty—Thomas Fleming, *Liberty! The American Revolution*

Morgan—Edmund Morgan, *Benjamin Franklin*

Schiff—Stacy Schiff, *A Great Improvisation*

'76—Henry Steele Commager & Richard B. Morris, *The Spirit of Seventy-Six*

Updike—John Updike, "The Founding Father"

Van Doren—Carl Van Doren, *Benjamin Franklin*

Wood—Gordon S. Wood, *The Americanization of Benjamin Franklin*

One: The Runaway Apprentice

Page

1   "I was dirty...have little": Autobiography, p. 75
     "well set and very strong": Autobiography, p. 54

1–3 "having no room...arouse me": Autobiography, p. 76

3   "several sly questions...next morning": Autobiography, p. 77

4   "Living near...manage boats": Autobiography, pp. 53–54

4–5 "a kind of sandals...pleasure imaginable": Van Doren, p. 17

5–6 "I was generally...not honest": Autobiography, p. 54

Page

6   "I do not remember...not read": Autobiography, p. 53

6–7 "break away...missed or wanted": Autobiography, pp. 57–59

7–8 "I had never...extremely ambitious": Autobiography, p. 62

8–9 "was excited...demeaned me too much": Autobiography, pp. 67–68

9   "Perhaps I was...provoking": Autobiography, p. 70
     "which I took...shortening it": Autobiography, p. 68
     "Printed and sold...are taken": Bowen, p. 32
     "His harsh...my freedom": Autobiography, pp. 69–70
     "As we had...in my pocket": Autobiography, p. 71

Two: Benjamin Franklin of Philadelphia, Printer

10   "I lived...as I could": Autobiography, p. 79
     "I endeavored...worked with": Autobiography, p. 78
     "lovers of reading...very pleasantly": Autobiography, p. 79
     "Many pleasant...we read": Autobiography, p. 90

10–11 "He said...succeed": Autobiography, p. 80

11   "saying many...so expensive": Autobiography, pp. 81–82
     "Since he...ready to go": Autobiography, pp. 86–87

12   "there was not...gave expectations": Autobiography, pp. 94–95
     "You will improve...greater advantage": Autobiography, p. 94
     "spent a good...amusement": Autobiography, p. 96
     "took great notice...topics": Autobiography, p. 97

12–13 "performing on the way...to see it": Autobiography, pp. 104–05

Page

14   "The industry...out of bed": Isaacson, p. 54
     "I took care...contrary": Autobiography, p. 125
     "was obtained...the tongue": Autobiography, p. 151
     "having turned...each other happy": Autobiography, pp. 128–29

15   "Pappy" and "my dear child": Isaacson, p. 81
     "many pleasant...and Sayings": Brands, p. 125
     "When you're good...to yourself": Updike, p. 113
     "Eat to please...and wise": Almanack, pp. 40, 38, 39

15–16 "the good...collectively": Isaacson, p. 102

16   "I wished...avoid the other": Autobiography, p. 148
     "Waste nothing...Socrates": Autobiography, pp. 149–50
     "A task...by another": Autobiography, p. 146

16–17 "with occasional...with me": Autobiography, p. 155

17   "which secured...profitable": Autobiography, p. 171
     "what I look...friendship": Brands, p. 129
     "*I Benjamin Franklin...Printer*": Bowen, p. 8

Three: Snatching Lightning from the Sky

18–19 "black clothes...from frosts": I. Bernard Cohen, *Benjamin Franklin's Experiments on Heat Absorption as a Function of Color* (*Isis*, Vol. 34, No. 5, Summer 1943), p. 404

19   "As we enjoy...generously": Morgan, p. 28
     "electricians": Brands, p. 191

20   "sparks, of fire": Bowen, p. 48
     "subject...new to me": Autobiography, p. 240

21   "I eagerly...new wonders": Autobiography, p. 241
     "this miraculous bottle": Wood, p. 63
     "electric fluid": Morgan, p. 12

Page

21 "electric battery" and "self-moving wheel": Brands, p. 193

"the wonderful effects of points": Bowen, p. 52

"I was never...alive": Brands, pp. 191–92

"little leisure for anything else": Wood, p. 63

"use discovered...humble": Bowen, p. 6

"Since they agree...be made": Morgan, p. 13

22 "Mr. Franklin's...reality": Morgan, p. 139

"silk is fitter...tearing": Brands, p. 202

23 "Let the reader...moment": Bowen, p. 72

"compliments...thunderstorms": Isaacson, p. 140

24 "how to secure...lightning": Isaacson, p. 141

"Thus without studying...honors": Autobiography, p. 209

"we are generally...praise": Wood, p. 65

Four: Following the Example of the Iroquois

25 "leisure during...on me": Autobiography, p. 196

"My ambition...unsolicited": Autobiography, p. 197

26 "penny postman": Van Doren, p.213

28 "It would be...advantageous": Brands, pp. 232–33

"the disunited states...convenient for them": Brands, p. 234

29 "singularly impressive...other men": Bowen, p. 122

"Look about...fortifications": Bowen, p. 127

"solemnly renewed": Isaacson, p. 160

30 "consider themselves...one interest": Wood, p. 78

"I am still...princes": Van Doren, p. 223

31 "Our answers...abusive": Wood, p. 79

"a dangerous...other country": Wood, p. 69

"B.F.'s view...by great people": Bowen, p. 157

Five: Dr. Fatsides in the Mother Country

32 "A fat old fellow": Van Doren, p. 272

33 "There was not...by sunshine": Autobiography, p. 207

34 "Conversation warms the mind": Updike, p. 108

"were present...the university": Wood, p. 87

Page

34 "Dr. Franklin...in America": Updike, p. 168

"air bath...whatsoever": Isaacson, p. 243

"enormous size...Dr. Fatsides": Isaacson, pp. 241-42

35 "dangerous man": Wood, p. 69

"a more thorough...strongly": Brands, p. 301

"face turns...wrath": Bowen, p. 155

"The regard...small pleasure": Morgan, p. 107

"It is an...plaintive kind": Isaacson, p. 266

36 "both time and patience": Wood, p. 89

"a crimson satin cloak...somebody": Van Doren, pp. 276-77

"long absence...expected": Bowen, p. 173

"They are...England": Wood, p. 91

36–37 "respect for...affection": Wood, p. 91

37 "tyranny and oppression": Isaacson, p. 202

"I have long...in America": Morgan, p. 123

"the happy...accompany me": Wood, p. 97

"thinner of people...London": Wood, p. 97

"a succession...arrival": Morgan, p. 130

38 "She sings...the world": Van Doren, p. 305

"I am not yet...stronger": Van Doren, p. 305

"Do we come...black hair": Benjamin Franklin, *A Narrative of the Late Massacres* (http://www.historycarper.com/resources/twobf3/massacre.htm)

39 "did me the honor...for some time": Isaacson, pp. 212–13

"The fighting...the city": Van Doren, p. 310

"villain" and "black heart": Van Doren, p. 311

"tyrannical and inhuman": Isaacson, p. 215

"All regard...at an end": Van Doren, p. 311

"I am now...my enemies": Van Doren, p. 316

Six: Becoming a Rebel

40 "the very best...amiable": Bowen, p. 177

"A few months...little family": Isaacson, p. 219

41 "informing...total separation": Wood, p. 117

41–42 "They were governed...very much altered": Morgan, p. 157

42 "as we...there": Isaacson, p. 230

"I do not...make one": Bowen, p. 219

Page

43 "Being born...to both": Isaacson, p. 246

"My company...chose it": Wood, p. 140

"to convert...distant people": Isaacson, p. 247

"A great empire...the edges": Benjamin Franklin, *Rules By Which a Great Empire May Be Reduced to a Small One* (http://www.history1700s.com/article1100.shtml)

44 "All the courtiers...entertainment": Isaacson, p. 277

"the true incendiary...government": Morgan, pp. 202–03

"forfeited...men": Wood, p. 146

"The Doctor...to appear": Isaacson, pp. 277–78

"I will...for this": Wood, p. 147

45 "Be assured...affection": Van Doren, p. 477

45–46 "I have seen...with them": Isaacson, p. 280

46 "We must control...them": Liberty, p. 86

"Every act...revolt": Morgan, p. 163

"reflect on...blood": Liberty, p. 86

"If by some...health": Wood, p. 148

47 "I came here...winter": Isaacson, pp. 282-83

"It seems...so happily": Van Doren, p. 503

"You are looked...with me": Isaacson, pp. 282–83

"destroyed...ministers": Wood, p. 151

Seven: Declaring Independence

48 "gulf weed": Van Doren, p. 522

49–50 "Dr. Franklin...events": Brands, p. 494

50 "My time...afternoon": Morgan, p. 220

"Words...no use": Isaacson, p. 296

"treated as the cause...prevent": Wood, p. 167

"He does not...backward": Wood, p. 155

51 "an enemy...country": Isaacson, p. 308

52 "From my infancy...affable": Van Doren, p. 537

"I have undertaken...for me": Van Doren, p. 544

"suffered...swelled": Isaacson, p. 306

53 "must starve...surrender": Morgan, p. 231

"our firm...withdraw": Brands, p. 508

Picture Credits

Selected Bibliography

"Writing has been of great use to me in the course of my life," Benjamin Franklin wrote in his autobiography. The Library of America's selection of his best-known writings, edited by J. A. Leo Lemay (New York: Library of America, 2005), runs to 1,639 pages and includes essays, political satires, pamphlets, speeches, personal letters, prefaces to *Poor Richard's Almanack*, and the famous autobiography.

Franklin began his autobiography late in life and worked on it at four different times over a period of nineteen years. Written in the mellow afterglow of memory, it is the essential source to his early years. It has been translated into a dozen languages, printed in more than 150 editions, and read by millions. My references are to the authoritative edition prepared by the editors of the Franklin Papers and based on the original handwritten manuscript: *The Autobiography of Benjamin Franklin*, Second Edition, edited by Leonard W. Labaree, Ralph L. Ketcham, Helen C. Boatfield, and Helene H. Fineman (New Haven: Yale University Press, 1964). My references to *Poor Richard's Almanack* are from *Wit and Wisdom from Poor Richard's Almanack* (Mineola, New York: Dover Publications, 1999).

I have drawn on three outstanding full-length biographies: Carl Van Doren's *Benjamin Franklin*, originally published in 1938 by the Viking Press and winner of the 1939 Pulitzer Prize, reissued in two volumes (Safety Harbor, FL: Simon Publications, 2002); H. W. Brands's *The First American: The Life and Times of Benjamin Franklin* (New York: Anchor Books, 2000), which draws on previously unpublished letters and other materials; and Walter Isaacson's *Benjamin Franklin: An American Life* (New York: Simon & Schuster, 2003), which is enlivened by an abundance of anecdotal material.

Two recent short biographies, each a penetrating character study, are Edmund S. Morgan's *Benjamin Franklin* (New Haven: Yale University Press, 2002) and Gordon S. Woods's *The Americanization of Benjamin Franklin* (New York: Penguin Press, 2004). Catherine Drinker Bowen's *The*

Most Dangerous Man in America: Scenes from the Life of Benjamin Franklin (Boston: Little, Brown, 1974) is an out-of-print classic that focuses on a sequence of key events in Franklin's life. Stacy Schiff's *A Great Improvisation: Franklin, France, and the Birth of America* (New York: Henry Holt, 2005) offers an illuminating portrait of Franklin and his critical diplomacy at the French court, which helped save the American Revolution.

John Updike's essay "The Founding Father" in *The New Yorker*, February 22, 1988, is a concise and rewarding appraisal of what Updike calls the "many Bens." Among the many informative narrative histories of the Revolutionary War, I drew especially on Thomas Fleming's *Liberty! The American Revolution* (New York: Viking, 1997). And as with my earlier books on the revolutionary period, I consulted Henry Steele Commager and Richard B. Morris's indispensible *The Spirit of 'Seventy-Six: The Story of the American Revolution as Told by Participants* (New York: Harper/Collins, 1975).

Illustration from an 1800 edition of Poor Richard's Almanack.

Index